A Beginner's Guide to

Kṛṣṇa Consciousness

Books by His Divine Grace A.C. Bhaktivedanta Swami Prabhupāda:

Bhagavad-gītā As It Is
Śrīmad-Bhāgavatam (18 vols.; with disciples)
Śrī Caitanya-caritāmṛta (9 vols.)
Kṛṣṇa, The Supreme Personality of Godhead
Teachings of Lord Caitanya
The Nectar of Devotion
The Nectar of Instruction
Śrī Īśopaniṣad
Light of the Bhāgavata
Easy Journey to Other Planets
The Science of Self-Realization
Kṛṣṇa Consciousness: The Topmost Yoga System
Perfect Questions, Perfect Answers
Teachings of Lord Kapila, the Son of Devahuti
Transcendental Teachings of Prahlāda Mahārāja
Teachings of Queen Kuntī
Kṛṣṇa, the Reservoir of Pleasure
The Path of Perfection
Life Comes from Life
Message of Godhead
The Perfection of Yoga
Beyond Birth and Death
On the Way to Kṛṣṇa
Rāja-vidyā: The King of Knowledge
Elevation to Kṛṣṇa Consciousness
Kṛṣṇa Consciousness: The Matchless Gift
The Nārada-bhakti-sūtra (with disciples)
The Mukunda-mālā-stotra (with disciples)
Introduction to Bhagavad-gītā
Back to Godhead magazine (founder)
A Second Chance
The Journey of Self-Discovery
The Laws of Nature
Renunciation Through Wisdom
Civilization & Transcendence
The Quest for Enlightenment
Beyond Illusion and Doubt
Dharma: The Way of Transcendence
The Hare Krishna Challenge

A Beginner's Guide to

Kṛṣṇa Consciousness

Bhakti Vikāsa Swami

The Bhaktivedanta Book Trust

Readers interested in the subject matter of this book are invited by The Bhaktivedanta Book Trust to correspond with its secretary at the following address:

The Bhaktivedanta Book Trust
Hare Krishna Land
Juhu, Mumbai 400 049, India

Website / E-mail :
www.indiabbt.com
admin@indiabbt.com

A Beginner's Guide to Kṛṣṇa Consciousness (English)

1st printing in India : 5,000 copies
2nd to 12th printings : 1,85,000 copies
13th printing, May 2022 : 30,000 copies

ISBN : 978-93-82716-69-3

Published and Printed
by The Bhaktivedanta Book Trust.

ET6N

Table of Contents

Dedication

This book is dedicated to its readers. If it helps you advance in Kṛṣṇa consciousness, please remember to bless me so that I can make some advancement.

Introduction

Human life is not meant for whimsical, mindless living but for understanding God. Kṛṣṇa is God, and He can be understood by the process of *bhakti* (devotional service). The most authorized path of *bhakti* for the present age of quarrel and hypocrisy (Kali-yuga) is that taught by Lord Caitanya Mahāprabhu.

Lord Caitanya is Kṛṣṇa Himself in the form of a devotee. He taught the easiest method for self-realization, the chanting of the Hare Kṛṣṇa *mahā-mantra*:

Hare Kṛṣṇa, Hare Kṛṣṇa,
Kṛṣṇa Kṛṣṇa, Hare Hare
Hare Rāma, Hare Rāma,
Rāma Rāma, Hare Hare

As Lord Caitanya predicted, this chanting is no longer confined to India but has spread all over the world. His Divine Grace A.C. Bhaktivedanta Swami Prabhupāda was empowered by Lord Caitanya to make this chanting process universally popular. In pursuance of the teachings of Lord Caitanya, Śrīla Prabhupāda founded the International Society for Krishna Consciousness in New York in 1966. Śrīla Prabhupāda passed away from this world in 1977, but the movement he started continues to grow.

Every day more and more people are taking interest in Kṛṣṇa consciousness. By reading the books of Śrīla Prabhupāda and associating with members of ISKCON, many feel inclined to take up Kṛṣṇa consciousness in their own lives.

The practice of Kṛṣṇa consciousness is simple, but to learn the techniques requires guidance. Such circumstances as living far from an ISKCON center make it hard for many people eager to take up Kṛṣṇa consciousness to do so properly because of insufficient personal instruction.

This book is especially meant for such persons. It is a practical guide on how to chant the holy names, worship at home, apply *tilaka*, observe festivals, and so on. Most instructions apply to all devotees, but some are especially meant for those living at home.

However, this book is not a substitute for personal supervision, which is essential for neophyte devotees to help raise them to the transcendental platform. Śrīla Prabhupāda writes: "For one who does not take personal training under the guidance of a bona fide spiritual master, it is impossible to even begin to understand Kṛṣṇa." (*Bhagavad-gītā* 11.54 purport). So this book cannot be more than a supplement to personal training. Even from a practical viewpoint, to properly learn the procedures of applying *tilaka*, performing *kīrtana*, etc., outlined in this book, one needs to see them done by experienced devotees.

The instructions in this book are based on the practices of the *Gauḍīya-Vaiṣṇava sampradāya* (the line of Vaiṣṇavas coming from Lord Caitanya), as described in such authorized books as *Hari-bhakti-vilāsa*, *Bhakti-rasāmṛta-sindhu*, and *Śrī Upadeśāmṛta*. More specifically, the instructions given here are based on the teachings of His Divine Grace A.C. Bhaktivedanta Swami Prabhupāda. Without deviating an inch from the previous *ācāryas* and timeless scriptures, Śrīla Prabhupāda presented Kṛṣṇa consciousness in a way just suitable for modern mankind.

Along with guidance on basic Vaiṣṇava practices, we have included some useful information for newcomers to Kṛṣṇa consciousness. However, we have not elaborately explained the philosophy of Kṛṣṇa consciousness because Śrīla Prabhupāda has exhaustively treated it in his books. This book is a practical guide for those who want to apply that philosophy in their own lives. But we strongly urge our readers to solidify the practices outlined here by studying Śrīla Prabhupāda's books every day.

In the beginning, these do's and don't's of Kṛṣṇa consciousness may seem intimidating. Newcomers need not feel discouraged, however. It is not expected that everyone can take up Kṛṣṇa consciousness fully all at once. One may take it up gradually. When aspiring devotees feel comfortable and confident with one step, they may take another. Kṛṣṇa consciousness is pleasing to the soul, and so anyone who sincerely takes it up will naturally feel encouraged to go deeper and make further progress.

Through the simple activities of Kṛṣṇa consciousness this guide describes, any person, regardless of age, caste, creed, gender, or education, can easily develop pure love of God, escape from the horrible cycle of birth and death, and enter the kingdom of God. The *saṅkīrtana* movement of Lord Caitanya Mahāprabhu is now offering this wonderful opportunity to everyone all over the world.

We humbly entreat the readers to take up Kṛṣṇa consciousness in all seriousness.

Lord Caitanya says: "Wake up, sleeping souls! How long will you sleep on the lap of the witch called *Māyā*? I have brought the medicine to cure your disease of material existence. It is the chanting of the holy names of the Lord:

Hare Kṛṣṇa, Hare Kṛṣṇa,
Kṛṣṇa Kṛṣṇa, Hare Hare
Hare Rāma, Hare Rāma,
Rāma Rāma, Hare Hare

"Now pray for this Hare Kṛṣṇa mantra and take it."

Why Practice Kṛṣṇa Consciousness?

We are not these bodies but spirit souls. The body is temporary but the soul (*jīvātmā*) residing in each body is eternal.

Each soul has an eternal, dynamic, blissful relationship with the Supreme Soul, the Supreme Personality of Godhead, Lord Kṛṣṇa. Our actual life is not in this material world but in the spiritual world with Kṛṣṇa.

Kṛṣṇa directly presides over the spiritual world. There He is surrounded by countless loving servitors who are all completely pure devotees, perfect beings with only one desire: to please Kṛṣṇa. They are totally free from mundane desires, lust, greed, and envy.

In the spiritual world, everything — the land, the trees, the homes, the water — is conscious and blissful. There is no sorrow but only enjoyment. Not the stale, false enjoyment of this material world, but meaningful spiritual ecstasy in relationship with Kṛṣṇa. Kṛṣṇa eternally performs wonderful variegated activities with His devotees. Life there is a constant festival of singing, dancing, playing, and eating with the Supreme Personality of Godhead.

Those souls who, out of madness, are inimical towards Kṛṣṇa are placed in the material world. This world is like a prison house for reformatory punishment. The conditioned souls here suffer repeated birth and death in 8,400,000 species of life. Influenced by *māyā* (illusion) and insane due to false prestige, the conditioned soul imagines himself happy even when in the body of a stool-eating hog. From the topmost planet to the lowest, this world is a great ocean of distress.

Kṛṣṇa does not want us to rot in the material world. He is calling us to come back to the spiritual world to live happily with Him forever. Those who are intelligent listen to Kṛṣṇa (as He speaks in *Bhagavad-gītā As It Is*) and try to make a solution to the problem of repeated birth and death. They take up devotional service to revive their dormant Kṛṣṇa consciousness and go back to Godhead.

In the present age, Kali-yuga, Kṛṣṇa Himself taught Kṛṣṇa consciousness in His most merciful incarnation Śrī Caitanya Mahāprabhu. Lord Caitanya inaugurated the *saṅkīrtana* movement, a movement centered on the congregational chanting of the Holy Names. *Saṅkīrtana* is the simplest and most joyful process for realizing God. It is *kevala ānanda-kanda*— simply joyful.

Kṛṣṇa consciousness is not a dull, dry, ritualistic religion. Kṛṣṇa consciousness means chanting the holy names, dancing in ecstasy, feasting on *kṛṣṇa-prasāda*, associating with saintly devotees, serving the Supreme Personality of Godhead in His Deity form, appreciating the unsurpassable beauty of the Deity, understanding profound philosophy, hearing about the potencies and pastimes of Kṛṣṇa, and preaching His glories. Kṛṣṇa consciousness means the mood of the spiritual world. It is a life of ever-increasing pleasure, and it ultimately brings us to the point where we can directly see Kṛṣṇa and speak with Him face to face.

Kṛṣṇa consciousness is the tried, tested, and proven method for achieving the perfection of life. Many persons in the past have become purified by Kṛṣṇa consciousness and have thus attained to Kṛṣṇa's lotus feet.

Those whose spiritual intelligence is awakened will appreciate the unsurpassed mercy Lord Caitanya is giving by inviting us to join His *saṅkīrtana* movement. Such persons take up Kṛṣṇa consciousness with all sincerity, determined to make this their last birth in the material world.

Even from the social or personal point of view, Kṛṣṇa consciousness is so wonderful that it is beneficial for everyone. Simply by practicing devotional service, devotees develop all good qualities. They become kind, tolerant, humble, self-controlled, peaceful, and pleasing to all. Kṛṣṇa consciousness even offers solutions to all economic, social, political, psychological, philosophical, and religious problems. How this is so is fully described in Śrīla Prabhupāda's books.

Therefore every thoughtful person should immediately take up Kṛṣṇa consciousness with full heart and soul.

The Basis: Guru, Sādhu, and Śāstra

"Śrīla Narottama dāsa Ṭhākura advises: *sādhu śāstra-guru-vākya, cittete kariyā aikya*. The meaning of this instruction is that one must consider the instructions of the *sādhu*, the revealed scriptures, and the spiritual master in order to understand the real purpose of spiritual life. Neither a *sādhu* (saintly person or Vaiṣṇava) nor a bona fide spiritual master says anything that is beyond the scope of the sanction of the revealed scriptures. Thus the statements of the revealed scriptures correspond to those of the bona fide spiritual master and saintly persons. One must therefore act with reference to these three important sources of understanding." (*Śrī Caitanya-caritāmṛta, Ādi-līlā* 7.48 purport)

The philosophy and practice of Kṛṣṇa consciousness are delineated by *guru*, *sādhu*, and *śāstra*. *Śāstra* (scripture) is the word of God or (equally valid) that which is spoken by realized devotees of God. *Śāstra* is strictly followed by *sadhus*, but only scriptures and commentaries accepted by Vaiṣṇavas can be considered properly authorized. The bona fide *guru*, one's personal teacher, knows the authorized Vaiṣṇava scriptures, lives according to their tenets, and teaches the same.

Kṛṣṇa consciousness is thus not to be approached whimsically. The Absolute Truth is not subject to opinions dreamed up in our tiny brains. That Absolute Truth of Kṛṣṇa consciousness is transmitted through the timeless and changeless system of devotional service. It is accepted by great authorities such as Lord Brahmā, Nārada, and Lord Śiva. That system of philosophy and practice is received even in the present day by the unbroken disciplic succession (*paramparā*).

Many people become enthusiastic to take up Kṛṣṇa consciousness and try to follow what they have seen devotees doing. But because they lack proper guidance and association they are unable to advance beyond the neophyte platform. Their understanding and practice of Kṛṣṇa consciousness are often faulty because of immaturity and the tendency to mix speculative ideas with the time-tested truths of pure devotional service.

For instance, a common diversion is to attempt to mix Kṛṣṇa consciousness with mundane knowledge, such as that derived from so-called academic scholars, scientists, psychologists, management experts, and so on. However, implicit in the mindset of all nondevotees is consciousness of sense gratification. All conditioned souls have the four defects of imperfect senses, being illusioned, making mistakes, and cheating.Therefore, devotees accept only liberated souls as authorities and do not take seriously the speculations of others.

In one sense, any beginning in Kṛṣṇa consciousness is good. But to be actually successful in devotional service a person must accept the authorized process. One must accept the guidance of a bona fide spiritual master with full submission. Simply thinking oneself religious or spiritual on the strength of a little practice will not be very helpful.

For those who want to start devotional service but have little chance of personal guidance, this book will, to a great extent, protect them from error and confusion. That is because it is based on the infallible ground of *guru*, *sādhu*, and *śāstra*. The reader will at least not have to speculate about how to put on *tilaka*, perform *saṅkīrtana*, etc. But again, stress must be given to accepting the shelter of a bona fide spiritual master, taking initiation from him, learning from him, and serving him in full submission.

Understanding Kṛṣṇa Consciousness As It Is

Everybody in India knows at least something about Kṛṣṇa. Unfortunately, certain unscrupulous persons have propagated many false concepts about Kṛṣṇa and about the process of *bhakti*. As a result, most Indians, despite their natural Kṛṣṇa conscious inclinations, are confused about the real understanding and practice of *kṛṣṇa-bhakti.* For them to take up Kṛṣṇa consciousness in the actual bona fide manner, they will have to accept that many of the ideas they have about Kṛṣṇa and Kṛṣṇa consciousness are erroneous and misleading.

Some of the most prominent misconceptions are as follows:

(1) Kṛṣṇa is a mythological figure. He did not (and does not) actually exist.

(2) Kṛṣṇa was a great man but not the Supreme Personality of Godhead.

(3) Kṛṣṇa was immoral.

(4) There are many gods; they are all the same, and worship of any of them is the same as worship of Kṛṣṇa.

(5) By meditation and spiritual practice anyone can become as good as Kṛṣṇa.

(6) It is not the person Kṛṣṇa who is to be worshiped but the unborn, eternal nature within Kṛṣṇa.

(7) When Kṛṣṇa is merciful to me, I shall surrender to Him.

(8) *Bhakti* is only a stepping-stone to *jñāna* (knowledge).

Although none of these ideas have either basis in reality or support from scripture, and are in fact completely fallacious, they have somehow or other become popular in Hindu society.

In India one will find dozens of fancy-sounding, erroneous theories like those mentioned above. These theories are propagated by envious people whose only business is to make a show of being religious. They divert their followers from the actual goal of religion, which is to surrender wholly and solely to Kṛṣṇa. As Kṛṣṇa Himself demands:

sarva-dharmān parityajya
mām ekaṁ śaraṇaṁ vraja
ahaṁ tvāṁ sarva-pāpebhyo
mokṣayiṣyāmi mā śucaḥ

"Abandon all varieties of religion and just surrender unto Me. I shall deliver you from all sinful reactions. Do not fear." (*Bhagavad-gītā* 18.66)

The propagators of false theories about Kṛṣṇa may appear to be pious and religious, but if they are asked to accept Kṛṣṇa as the Supreme Personality of Godhead, the primeval cause of all causes, and to surrender unto Him, they bluntly refuse. Kṛṣṇa describes such persons in the *Bhagavad-gītā* (7.15):

na māṁ duṣkṛtino mūḍhāḥ
prapadyante narādhamāḥ
māyayāpahṛta-jñānā
āsuraṁ bhāvam āśritāḥ

"Those miscreants who are grossly foolish, who are lowest among mankind, whose knowledge is stolen by illusion, and who partake of the atheistic nature of demons do not surrender unto Me."[1]

Anyone interested in becoming a pure devotee must always guard against contamination from nondevotees and false devotees.

The two main deviations from pure devotional service

[1] Śrīla Prabhupāda said, "This verse is very important."

are the Māyāvāda doctrine and sahajiyāism. Māyāvādīs are impersonalists: they refuse to accept the Personality of Kṛṣṇa as the Absolute Truth. Their aim is "to merge with God."

Lord Caitanya Mahāprabhu clearly said, *māyāvādī kṛṣṇe aparādhī:* "Māyāvādīs are offenders to Kṛṣṇa." (*Caitanya-caritāmṛta, Madhya-līlā* 17.129). Śrīla Prabhupāda explains why: "By . . . covering the glories of the Supreme Lord, the Māyāvādī philosophers have done the greatest disservice to human society." (*Caitanya-caritāmṛta, Ādi-līlā* 7.120, purport). "The Māyāvādīs' primary occupation is to offend the Supreme Personality of Godhead, Kṛṣṇa." (*Caitanya-caritāmṛta, Ādi-līlā* 7.144, purport).

Unfortunately, Māyāvāda philosophy is almost all-pervasive in modern Indian thought. Śrīla Prabhupāda said that "Impersonalism has killed India's Vedic culture." (Conversation, 5 July 1976).

Bhakti means surrender to Kṛṣṇa based on acceptance of His supremacy, His transcendental personality, and His eternal spiritual form. But Māyāvādīs preposterously equate ordinary living beings with God, undermining the very basis of *bhakti*. Lord Caitanya Mahāprabhu therefore warned that anyone who hears Māyāvāda explanations of scripture is doomed; his spiritual life is ruined.

Sahajiyās are pseudodevotees who take devotional service cheaply. Without following the standard rules and regulations of devotional service, they consider themselves highly advanced, making a show of intense devotion.

Unscrupulous professional speakers, *bhajan* singers, comic-book publishers, and false *gurus* have commercialized Kṛṣṇa consciousness among the masses. Although they may speak or sing of Kṛṣṇa very attractively, their motive is simply to make money.

Some of these so-called *sadhus* collect many followers by their personal charisma. However, they have nothing substantial to offer. Such cheaters are interested only in money and fame. They entertain their followers with many stories but hardly care to teach them philosophy. They are not strict with their disciples and more or less let them do as they please. Expert showmen, they entice people with talks of advanced devotion. Both the so-called *guru* and his so-called disciples, although materially motivated, float in an illusion of being highly advanced. Factually, they are all full of lust, greed, envy, and illusion and are fully attracted to material life. Insincere people who want to be cheated are easily misled by such expert cheaters. Intelligent people who are seriously interested in pure devotional service should search out a genuine *sadhu*, whose instruction will actually help them become purified and free from material attachments by guiding them in the performance of regulated devotional service.

Another class of pseudo-religionists emphasize worldly philanthropy, such as opening hospitals and schools and feeding the poor. However, genuine *sadhus* know that such mundane welfare work is of no ultimate value, for until a person becomes enlightened in Kṛṣṇa consciousness he is doomed to continue rotating in the ghastly cycle of birth and death and suffering its concomitant miseries. Therefore the real duty of a *sadhu* is to bring people to Kṛṣṇa consciousness; those who equate worldly service with spiritual service simply cheat others while purporting to benefit them.

In addition to the bogus *sadhus* and their followers, there are many devotees who, despite belonging to authorized Vaiṣṇava traditions, have compromised their beliefs and practices and thus lost the essential spirit of surrender to Viṣṇu.

Another problem in this Age of *Kali* is the prevalence of innumerable false incarnations of God. The perverted atmosphere of this age has allowed these pseudo-incarnations to influence foolish people to such an extent that worshiping them is often more popular than worshiping the real God (Kṛṣṇa). And their bewildered followers take the meaningless pronouncements of such "Gods" as sacred philosophy.

All these nondevotees, semidevotees, and pseudo-devotees may appear to be practicing *bhakti*, but because they are misinformed, misdirected, materially motivated, or envious of Kṛṣṇa, all their prayers, *mantras*, and *pūjās* are useless. Their activities are not accepted as actual *bhakti* by real *paramparā* devotees.

In the words of Śrīla Rūpa Gosvāmī,

śruti-smṛti-purāṇādi-
pañcarātra-vidhiṁ vinā
aikāntikī harer bhaktir
utpātāyaiva kalpate

"Devotional service to the Lord that ignores the authorized books like the *Upaniṣads, Purāṇas, Nārada Pañcarātra*, etc., is simply an unnecessary disturbance in society." (*Bhakti-rasāmṛta-sindhu* 1.2.101).

Modern Indian religious culture is overrun by all manner of whimsical, distorted, and imaginary beliefs and rituals. So-called yogis, swamis, *gurus*, babas, incarnations, miracle workers, fakirs, and countless other "godmen" teach all varieties of questionable theories, instructing their followers in everything — except surrender to Kṛṣṇa, the Supreme Personality of Godhead. Bogus religion has thus all but swamped genuine, authorized, and bona fide philosophy and practices. To the untrained, the difference between the genuine, the partially genuine, and the false is not readily apparent. Superficially, Kṛṣṇa consciousness appears like another "Hindu group." As in Kṛṣṇa consciousness, many groups have their own *bhajans*, temples, festivals, scriptures, *gurus*, *tilaka*, and so on. Therefore the innocent public, without going deep into the matter, often concludes that "all paths are the same."

But there is a vast difference between the path of pure devotional service to Kṛṣṇa and all other paths. The difference is that Kṛṣṇa consciousness is the only factual and complete reality, as enunciated in the revealed scriptures and accepted by all authorities. Only Kṛṣṇa consciousness (especially as taught in the line of Lord Caitanya) teaches one how to be free from all personal motives and thus attain one's constitutional position as an eternal servant of Kṛṣṇa, the Supreme Personality of Godhead.

Śrīla Rūpa Gosvāmī has defined this superlative standard thus:

anyābhilāṣitā-śūnyaṁ
jñāna-karmādy-anāvṛtam

ānukūlyena kṛṣṇānu-
śīlanaṁ bhaktir uttamā

"One should render transcendental loving service to the Supreme Lord, Kṛṣṇa, favorably, without desire for material profit or gain through fruitive activities or philosophical speculation. That is called pure devotional service." (*Bhakti-rasāmṛta-sindhu* 1.1.11)

It is vital for every aspiring candidate in Kṛṣṇa consciousness to understand the essential difference between pure Kṛṣṇa consciousness and every other path.

The Kṛṣṇa consciousness movement is not just another "Hindu sect," nor is it just "another opinion." The Kṛṣṇa consciousness movement of Lord Caitanya Mahāprabhu is a cultural, philosophical, and scientific presentation meant for the respiritualization of the entire world. It is destined to go down in the annals of history as having saved human society in its darkest hour.[2] "Kṛṣṇa consciousness is a serious education, not an ordinary religion." (The Science of Self-Realization). "[The] Kṛṣṇa consciousness movement is genuine, historically authorized, natural, and transcendental due to its being based on *Bhagavad-gītā As It Is*. It is gradually becoming the most popular movement in the entire world." (*Bhagavad-gītā As It Is*, Preface). "This Krishna Consciousness movement is meant for a complete overhauling of the whole social, political, religious, moral, educational, and hygienic principles." (Śrīla Prabhupāda letter, 18 January 1969). "Our program is sublime. Our philosophy is practical and authorized; our character, the

[2] This and the previous sentence are paraphrased quotes from Śrīla Prabhupāda.

purest; our program, the simplest; but our ultimate goal is the highest." (Śrīla Prabhupāda letter, 19 March 1970).

Therefore Kṛṣṇa consciousness is not just another "faith" derived from some poorly informed religious sentiment. It is the science of the Absolute Truth, being taught now as it has been since time immemorial — because truth never changes, nor is it subject to the adjustments of seasonal fashions. Kṛṣṇa consciousness is reality distinguished from illusion, truth distinguished from falsehood, light distinguished from darkness. Attainment of Kṛṣṇa consciousness is the highest perfection, not even slightly comparable to any particular faith or philosophy of this material world.

Without developing a clear philosophical understanding of the unique purity of Kṛṣṇa consciousness, a devotee will not be able to advance properly, even if he learns the techniques of devotional service outlined in this book. A change of heart is required.

Of course, activities in Kṛṣṇa consciousness are always beneficial, but to make rapid advancement one must give up attachment to mundane religious processes. As Kṛṣṇa says in the *Bhagavad-gītā* (18.66):

sarva-dharmān parityajya
mām ekaṁ śaraṇaṁ vraja
ahaṁ tvāṁ sarva-pāpebhyo
mokṣayiṣyāmi mā śucaḥ

"Abandon all varieties of religion and just surrender unto Me. I shall deliver you from all sinful reactions. Do not fear."

To distinguish between what is genuine and what is bogus requires training, especially for those deeply steeped in devious misconceptions. The best program, therefore, is to study Śrīla Prabhupāda's books repeatedly and thoroughly. (Even if one cannot read many books, *Bhagavad-gītā As It Is* will suffice to eradicate all doubts, for in this one book Śrīla Prabhupāda has conclusively delineated the superiority of pure devotional service and the inferiority of all other paths).

One should also associate with devotees who are firmly fixed up in Kṛṣṇa consciousness, being free from all sentimental attachments to cheating in the name of religion.

Some quotes from Śrīla Prabhupāda on these matters appear below:

> "Śrīla Rūpa Gosvāmī advises...that devotees who have already tasted the nectar of devotion be very careful to protect devotional service from dry speculators, formal ritualistic elevationists, and impersonal salvationists. Devotees should protect their valuable jewel of spiritual love from the clutches of thieves and burglars. In other words, a pure devotee should not describe devotional service and its different analytical aspects to dry speculators and false renouncers. Those who are not devotees can never achieve the benefits of devotional service. For them the subject of devotional service is always very difficult to understand. Only persons who have dedicated their lives unto the lotus feet of the Supreme Personality of Godhead can

relish the real nectar of devotion." (*The Nectar of Devotion*, Chapter 34)

"The fact is that I am the only [person] in India who is openly criticising not only demigod worship and impersonalism but everything that falls short of complete surrender to Krishna. My *Guru* Maharaja never compromised in his preaching, nor will I, nor should any of my students." (Śrīla Prabhupāda's letter, 3 January 1972).

The Significance of Śrīla Prabhupāda

The honorific title "Prabhupāda" is properly used for designating those exceptionally great spiritual masters who have made an outstanding contribution of literature or preaching to the world. Examples are Śrīla Rūpa Gosvāmī Prabhupāda, Śrīla Jīva Gosvāmī Prabhupāda, and Śrīla Bhaktisiddhānta Sarasvatī Gosvāmī Prabhupāda.

When members of ISKCON speak of "Prabhupāda" they refer to His Divine Grace A.C. Bhaktivedanta Swami Prabhupāda, who is also correctly addressed as "Śrīla Prabhupāda," for he occupies a unique position in the religious history of the world.

In *Śrīmad-Bhāgavatam* (1.5.11) Śrīla Vyāsadeva states that the *Bhāgavatam* is "meant to bring about a revolution in the impious life of a misdirected civilization." Learned Vaiṣṇava scholars have discerned that this statement of Vyāsadeva's must refer to the preaching mission brought about by Śrīla A.C. Bhaktivedanta Swami Prabhupāda. It was he only who, five thousand years after Śrīla Vyāsadeva's compilation of the *Bhāgavatam*, wrote his Bhaktivedanta purports on *Bhāgavatam* as his most important contribution toward the revolutionary respiritualization of the entire human society, which was lost in the darkness of materialism.

Also, Lord Caitanya Mahāprabhu predicted that His holy name would be broadcast in every town and village of the world. Ācāryas of His *sampradāya* predicted that the spread of Kṛṣṇa consciousness would usher in a ten-thousand-year Golden Age within the dark Age of Kali. And in the *Caitanya-maṅgala*, Locana Dāsa Ṭhākura foretold that a great *senapati* (general) would appear in order to widely and powerfully preach Lord Caitanya's message. That confidential task of spreading Kṛṣṇa consciousness all over the world was entrusted to His Divine Grace A.C. Bhaktivedanta Swami Prabhupāda.

Śrī Caitanya-caritāmṛta confirms that only one who is empowered by Kṛṣṇa can infuse Kṛṣṇa consciousness into the hearts of the masses. The great Vaiṣṇava *ācārya* Śrīla Bhaktivinoda Ṭhākura (1838–1914) predicted that "very soon a great personality will appear who will spread Kṛṣṇa consciousness all over the world." That person is clearly His Divine Grace A.C. Bhaktivedanta Swami Prabhupāda.

Bhaktivinoda Ṭhākura also said that a Vaiṣṇava's greatness can be understood by seeing how many nondevotees he converts to Vaiṣṇavism. To bring even one highly qualified person to Kṛṣṇa consciousness is difficult. But Śrīla Prabhupāda was so empowered by Kṛṣṇa that he went among the most unlikely candidates — the hedonistic youth of the Western countries — and made devotees by the thousands. No one can fully understand the extraordinary task Śrīla Prabhupāda performed. He went alone among persons who were far removed from Vedic culture, who had no idea of how to receive a *sadhu*, and who had been raised in a society that vigorously promotes meat-eating, illicit sex, gambling, and intoxication,. They were almost completely unqualified as candidates for spiritual life.

Yet Śrīla Prabhupāda not only went among such people, but he gradually managed to train many of them to such an extent that they are now accepted everywhere as first-class Vaiṣṇavas and preachers, qualified to impart Kṛṣṇa consciousness to others.

There were certainly many Vaiṣṇavas in India who were devoted, learned, and renounced. But the fact remains that only Śrīla Prabhupāda was sufficiently qualified to spread Kṛṣṇa consciousness all over the world. Only he had sufficient faith in Lord Caitanya's instructions, his spiritual master's order, and Kṛṣṇa's holy name to seriously attempt spreading Kṛṣṇa consciousness outside India. Only he had that much compassion and vision to preach the message of Lord Caitanya to those who most needed it. Only one of Kṛṣṇa's topmost confidential devotees could perform such an extraordinary task. From his unparalleled achievements it is clear that Śrīla Prabhupāda occupies a unique position in the history of Vaiṣṇavism.

Śrīla Prabhupāda was empowered to spread Kṛṣṇa consciousness in a practical and straightforward way, just suitable for the modern world. Without compromising the teachings of Kṛṣṇa consciousness even slightly, he preserved its esoteric truths in a clear manner suitable for both the layman and the scholar.

Śrīla Prabhupāda personally oversaw the development of ISKCON. He personally set up the programs that were to form the basis of ISKCON's expansion: production and distribution of transcendental books, *harināma-saṅkīrtana*, temples and ashrams, *prasāda* distribution, transcendental farm communities, *gurukulas*, preaching to scientists and scholars, etc.

Śrīla Prabhupāda gave comprehensive directions in every aspect of Kṛṣṇa consciousness: *sādhana*, preaching, Deity worship, cooking for Kṛṣṇa, *mantra* recitation. He even demonstrated such details as how to wear a *dhotī*.

Śrīla Prabhupāda is thus the Founder-*Ācārya* of ISKCON. Whatever standards and instructions we have in ISKCON come from him. Therefore, Śrīla Prabhupāda will always remain the main *śikṣā-guru* and *ācārya* of ISKCON.

Both scripture and tradition offer various approaches to Kṛṣṇa consciousness, but followers of Śrīla Prabhupāda execute Kṛṣṇa consciousness as he showed them, knowing that Śrīla Prabhupāda, as a faithful follower of his *guru* and the previous *ācāryas*, presented Kṛṣṇa consciousness in the best way for the modern age.

Śrīla Prabhupāda's success indicate that his endeavors are ordained and blessed by the Supreme Lord Kṛṣṇa Himself.

Śrīla Prabhupāda gave certain instructions that are absolutely necessary for initiated disciples to follow if they at all wish to claim to be "his genuine or serious devotees". For instance, Śrīla Prabhupāda demanded that initiated devotees rise by 4:00 a.m., attend *maṅgala-ārati*, chant at least sixteen rounds of the *mahā-mantra* every day, and undeviatingly follow the four regulative principles.

All such standards that Śrīla Prabhupāda clearly defined are the standards to be followed in ISKCON. A rightly situated, successful follower of Śrīla Prabhupāda is simply a faithful standard-bearer. He does not try to change or interpret the standards and programs Śrīla Prabhupāda gave, for he knows that what Śrīla Prabhupāda gave us is perfectly complete and completely perfect for the respiritualization of the entire human society — not only now, but for the next ten thousand years.

The Guru and Initiation

No one can become self-realized simply by reading books. Getting extracted from *māyā's* clutches is not easy. It is a path on which tests and difficulties are certain. No one can enter the kingdom of God on his own strength alone. Therefore, all the scriptures emphatically state the absolute necessity for all spiritual aspirants to accept the shelter of a bona fide spiritual master.

Śrīla Prabhupāda has said: "In every step of one's life the spiritual master guides…To give such guidance a spiritual master should be a very perfect man. Otherwise, how can he guide? . . . One cannot deny the order of the spiritual master. Therefore, one has to select a spiritual master by whose orders one will not commit a mistake. Suppose you accept the wrong person as a spiritual master and he guides you wrongly. Then your whole life is spoiled. So one has to select a spiritual master whose guidance will make one's life perfect. That is the relationship between spiritual master and disciple. It is not a formality. It is a great responsibility, both for the disciple and for the spiritual master." (From a lecture given in 1966).

Within ISKCON at the present time, any disciple of Śrīla Prabhupāda who is in good standing within the society and is approved to give initiation according to the society's procedures may be approached and requested to initiate a candidate into Kṛṣṇa consciousness.

"In good standing" means that he must have a clean record of following the regulative principles, daily chanting sixteen rounds of the Hare Kṛṣṇa *mahā-mantra* on *japa-mālā*, a good record of rising early and attending temple programs, steadiness in devotional service, and philosophical fidelity to the tenets of Kṛṣṇa consciousness, and he must be working within the organizational framework of ISKCON as accepted by the Governing Body Commission.

According to the *Hari-bhakti-vilāsa*, a candidate for Kṛṣṇa consciousness should regularly hear about Kṛṣṇa from a recognized devotee for at least a year. During this period, a relationship of *guru* and disciple may develop by service and enquiry. Then, if the disciple feels confident that "Here is a person to whom I can surrender, who can lead me to Kṛṣṇa," he may approach that devotee and pray to him for shelter and, ultimately, initiation.

The procedure for initiation in ISKCON, as presently directed by the GBC body, is both in line with scripture and suitable for a large organization whose *gurus* are often travelling and have wide areas of responsibility. Scriptures warn against hasty, rushed initiations, so a system of checks and balances is required to protect both *gurus* and disciples.

When a person, after coming in contact with ISKCON devotees, gets the divine inspiration to take up Kṛṣṇa consciousness seriously, he is first directed to follow Śrīla Prabhupāda's instructions. Śrīla Prabhupāda is the main *śikṣā-guru* (instructing spiritual master) and ***ācārya*** for all ISKCON members, and new devotees are taught to direct their guru-worship toward him. When offering obeisances or when offering food to Kṛṣṇa, they recite Śrīla Prabhupāda's *praṇāma-mantra*.

After practicing Kṛṣṇa consciousness according to the minimum standard (sixteen rounds of *japa* per day and following the four regulative principles) for at least six months, devotees may approach an ISKCON initiating *guru* and formally request to take shelter of him.

Approaching a *guru* should not be done "mechanically," but with faith and knowledge. By studying Śrīla Prabhupāda's books and consulting senior devotees, one should come to understand what the qualifications of a bona fide spiritual master are.

One should actually feel inspired by the devotee he is taking shelter of. One should be confident that "this devotee is a strict and faithful follower of Śrīla Prabhupāda who will guide me according to Śrīla Prabhupāda's instructions."

When one actually has this faith and confidence in a particular initiating *guru*, he may approach him for shelter. If a devotee feels that he needs it, he may take more time (than the stipulated minimum six months) to approach an initiating *guru*. There is no rush. Acceptance of a *guru* is perhaps the most important decision one will take in many life times.

Whoever one accepts as a *guru* in ISKCON will give the same basic instructions as those Śrīla Prabhupāda gave us: rise early, chant sixteen rounds, etc. However, the *guru* is a personal link to the *paramparā*, and prospective disciples are strongly recommended to be thoughtful in the matter of accepting a *guru*. Although they may take advice from senior devotees, they should also personally scrutinize the character of a devotee from whom they are considering accepting initiation.

Apart from the guidelines given above (for a devotee in "good standing" within ISKCON), one should see how much the *guru* has controlled the six urges, has developed the six positive qualities, and is free from the six faults (see *The Nectar of Instruction*, verses 1–3, for a detailed explanation).

Ideally, the *guru* should be learned in scripture and have a renounced attitude. Even if he has all facilities to use in Kṛṣṇa's service, he should not be attached to material comforts and opulence.

Furthermore, a disciple should see how much a spiritual master is attached to the process of devotional service and the preaching of Kṛṣṇa consciousness. It should also be understood that for a *guru* to have a big position and many followers is not necessarily indicative of his advancement in Kṛṣṇa consciousness or his ability to train disciples in devotional service.

The *guru*-disciple relationship is, ideally, close and personal. Therefore, when selecting the person who is to be one's spiritual master, one's worshipable guide, there are personal considerations also. The teachings of all bona fide spiritual masters are the same, but each spiritual master has his own personality and approach to guruship. For example, some *gurus* accept a few disciples and train them personally; others accept many disciples and delegate much of the responsibility for training to other senior devotees.

Be careful of being pressured into accepting initiation by over-zealous disciples of any particular *guru*. That is not the correct process. Those coming to ISKCON for spiritual shelter are entitled to approach any duly qualified and authorized member of the society to request initiation.

Having formally accepted the shelter of a *guru*, the devotee continues practicing Kṛṣṇa consciousness as before. However, he now directs his *guru*-worship toward the *guru* he is taking shelter of, as well as toward Śrīla Prabhupāda. He will now chant his own *guru's praṇāma-mantra* (if any) when offering obeisances to his *guru* or when offering food to Kṛṣṇa. Although he is not yet formally initiated, he has accepted shelter of a particular *guru* and starts to respect him as such.

At least six months after having formally taken shelter of a *guru*, a devotee may be initiated by him. Before an ISKCON *guru* can initiate a devotee, he must get a recommendation from the Temple President under whom that devotee is serving. Recommendation is based on (1) the devotee's passing of both written and oral tests administered by the Temple President (which show that the devotee understands the meaning of being a disciple, being a member of ISKCON, and other important philosophical points); and (2) the Temple President's personal verification of the disciple's chanting at least sixteen rounds of japa every day and strictly following the four regulative principles; and of his resolve to continue strictly practicing Kṛṣṇa consciousness throughout his life.

At initiation, the *guru* awards the disciple a spiritual name. If the disciple continues steadily in devotional service for at least six months more, he may, after going through procedures similar to those outlined above, be awarded brahminical initiation and Gāyatrī *mantras*.

Although thoughtfulness is required in the matter of initiation, waiting an inordinately long time is also not generally recommended. Usually, those who follow the four regulative principles and daily chant sixteen rounds of the *mahā-mantra* (especially those engaged in full-time temple service) accept initiation within one to two years of having taken up the process.

Apart from one's own initiating spiritual master, one should continue to hear from and serve other devotees (especially senior devotees) in ISKCON. Although it is natural that one will have affection for his own *guru*, the Vaiṣṇava etiquette is that one should treat the *guru's* Godbrothers as respectfully as the *guru* himself.

If one has previously taken initiation from a person who is not a bona fide, recognized Vaiṣṇava, then according to scripture that person must be rejected for the sake of accepting a bona fide spiritual master. People who already have such "*gurus*" are often afraid to give them up, fearing retribution, but they need not worry. The scriptural warning against leaving one's spiritual master does not apply in the case of bogus *gurus*, and this is stated in the scripture itself. Those who take shelter of a proper Vaiṣṇava *guru* will certainly be directly protected by Kṛṣṇa (see Śrīla Prabhupāda's purport to *Śrīmad-Bhāgavatam* 8.20.1 for further discussion of this point).

The Spiritual Master and the Disciple, published by the Bhaktivedanta Book Trust, is a comprehensive series of extracts from Śrīla Prabhupāda's books on this important subject of the guru-disciple relationship. It is recommended that every devotee carefully study this book before taking initiation.

The Need for Sādhana

Every living being is by nature Kṛṣṇa conscious. Due to *māyā* (illusion) we are now forgetful of Kṛṣṇa. *Sādhana* is the process for awakening our dormant Kṛṣṇa consciousness. It may be compared to the development of a baby. A baby has latent abilities to walk, talk, and do so many other things, which develop with time and training.

Sādhana is for devotees who are serious about understanding Kṛṣṇa and who know that without *sādhana* there is no actual spiritual life at all.

Sādhana means "spiritual practice." In *bhakti-yoga* (Kṛṣṇa consciousness) *sādhana* is centered on hearing and chanting about Kṛṣṇa. These act powerfully to purify our contaminated hearts and bring us gradually closer to Kṛṣṇa.

Sādhana should be practiced strictly and seriously, not just now and then, but every day. This kind of practice gives us the spiritual strength to resist the temptations of *māyā*. Without such dedication to *sādhana*, it is almost impossible to make solid advancement in Kṛṣṇa consciousness. Even if we have some feeling for Kṛṣṇa, without *sādhana* our devotional service will not develop beyond the superficial level.

Śrīla Prabhupāda established daily morning and evening programs of *sādhana* in his temples. One begins the morning program by rising by four a.m. at the latest. Early rising is imperative for serious devotees, because the early hours before dawn are the best time for spiritual practice.

After rising, devotees bathe, don fresh clothes, go to the temple, attend *maṅgala-ārati* and *Tulasī-ārati*, chant Hare Kṛṣṇa *mahā-mantra japa* on beads, join together in greeting the Deity and performing *guru-pūjā*, and hear *Śrīmad-Bhāgavatam* class. Thus the morning program lasts four to four and a half hours.

The evening program of *ārati* and *Bhagavad-gītā* class lasts about one and a half hours. Thus Śrīla Prabhupāda wanted his disciples to come together for *sādhana* for about six hours a day.

Devotees who live at home, or who are otherwise very busy, may think it impractical to spend so much time performing *sādhana*. In the rush and bustle of modern life, few people seem to have time for any thing but working and looking after their families. But life without a higher purpose is no better than that of the animals. In actual human life, spiritual practices are top priority and activities for bodily maintenance are secondary.

Those who have understood the importance of Kṛṣṇa consciousness — who know that without devotional service life is meaningless — will naturally want to arrange their lives to somehow or other incorporate time for *sādhana*.

This may mean re-organizing one's life. It may mean working fewer hours, reducing one's income to spend more time earning spiritual merit. In families where both husband and wife have outside jobs, it is definitely worth considering having the wife relinquish her job to stay back and attend to domestic affairs.

Even if we do not make such major changes in our lives, we can better use whatever time we have at our disposal. Most people waste precious hours in useless frivolities like gossiping and watching television. Better to save time for Kṛṣṇa conscious *sādhana*.

This book teaches how to practice *sādhana*. The section called "The Daily Schedule" gives an outline for an intensive *sādhana* program. Readers are urged to take up these practices in their daily lives, as much as possible, so as to quickly achieve the ultimate goal: pure love of Kṛṣṇa.

Kīrtana

harer nāma harer nāma harer nāmaiva kevalam
kalau nāsty eva nāsty eva nāsty eva gatir anyathā

"In this age of quarrel and hypocrisy, the only means of deliverance is the chanting of the holy names of the Lord. There is no other way. There is no other way. There is no other way." (*Bṛhan-nāradīya Purāṇa*)

hare kṛṣṇa hare kṛṣṇa kṛṣṇa kṛṣṇa hare hare
hare rāma hare rāma rāma rāma hare hare
iti ṣoḍaśakaṁ nāmnāṁ kali-kalmaṣa nāśanam
nātaḥ paratAropāyaḥ sarva-vedeṣu dṛśyate

"These sixteen names of the Hare Kṛṣṇa mantra are the only means to counteract the evil effects of Kali-yuga. In all the *Vedas* it is seen that to cross the ocean of nescience there is no alternative to the chanting of the holy name." (*Kali-santaraṇa Upaniṣad*)

Chanting the holy names of Hari is the *yuga-dharma* (recommended religious process of the age) for Kali-yuga. The importance of this chanting cannot be stressed too much. Everyone should chant these holy names as much as possible.

There are two ways of chanting: loudly, usually to the accompaniment of *mṛdaṅga* drums and *karatālas* (this is called *kīrtana*), and softly, mostly for oneself to hear (this is called *japa*).

Kīrtana is simple to perform. Among a group of devotees, one leads the *kīrtana*. That is, he sings first. Then the other devotees follow, that is, they sing the same words in unison to the same tune. Generally, the tunes sung are simple so that everyone can easily follow.

As described above, the most important *mantra* is the *mahā-mantra*: Hare Kṛṣṇa, Hare Kṛṣṇa, Kṛṣṇa Kṛṣṇa, Hare Hare/Hare Rāma, Hare Rāma, Rāma Rāma, Hare Hare.

This means, "Oh Kṛṣṇa, Oh energy of Kṛṣṇa, please engage me in Your service." *Hare* refers to the internal energy of Kṛṣṇa, Harā (Śrīmati Rādhārāṇi). Kṛṣṇa and Rāma are the principal names of the all-attractive Supreme Personality of Godhead, the reservoir of pleasure.

In our *kīrtanas*, the *mahā-mantra* should be chanted most of the time, as taught by Lord Caitanya Mahāprabhu. However, before chanting the *mahā-mantra*, we should chant Śrīla Prabhupāda's *praṇāma mantra* (see "Songs") and the Pañca-tattva *mahā-mantra* : *śrī-kṛṣṇa-caitanya prabhu-nityānanda/śrī-advaita gadādhara śrīvāsādi-gaura-bhakta vṛnda.*

The Pañca-tattva *mantra* is chanted before the Hare Kṛṣṇa *mahā-mantra* to invoke the mercy of Lord Caitanya and His associates and thus help us overcome offences incurred while chanting Hare Kṛṣṇa.

There are also many authorized *bhajans* and *mantras* composed by great devotees. These songs enhance devotional moods, and it is good for devotees to learn at least a few of the most important Vaiṣṇava *bhajans*, especially those in *Songs of the Vaiṣṇava Ācāryas*, a book published by the Bhaktivedanta Book Trust.

Japa

kṛṣṇa-nāma-mahā-mantrera ei ta' svabhāva
yei jape, tāra kṛṣṇe upajaye bhāva

"It is the nature of the Hare Kṛṣṇa *mahā-mantra* that anyone who chants it immediately develops his loving ecstasy for Kṛṣṇa." (*Caitanya-caritāmṛta, Ādi-līlā* 7.83)

Chanting Hare Kṛṣṇa *mahā-mantra japa* is essential for every serious devotee of Kṛṣṇa. Even though we may be busy with many duties, we must put aside some time every day for chanting Hare Kṛṣṇa.

Japa is best chanted on a *japa-mālā*, to keep count of the number of times we are chanting. His Divine Grace A.C. Bhaktivedanta Swami Prabhupāda, Founder-*Ācārya* of ISKCON and empowered propagator of the holy name in the present age, fixed sixteen rounds (16 x 108 chants of the Hare Kṛṣṇa mantra) as the minimum for initiated devotees.

Some newcomers to Kṛṣṇa consciousness find it difficult to chant sixteen rounds daily. Such persons may start by chanting fewer rounds daily: eight, four, two, or at the very least one, according to their capacity. Then, as they become accustomed to chanting, they may increase the number of rounds chanted daily, until they reach sixteen.

Never decrease the number of rounds chanted daily. After taking initiation, never chant fewer than sixteen rounds every day.

However, chanting *japa* is not simply a matter of finishing a certain number of rounds. Chanting with quality will help us make rapid spiritual advancement. One should chant *japa* distinctly, with feeling, praying to Kṛṣṇa and concentrating on hearing His holy name.

The best *japa-mālās* are made of Tulasī wood. Neem wood is also popular. As mentioned above, the *mālās* enable us to count the number of times we chant. The *japa-mālā* has 108 beads for counting on and one extra, which is called the "head bead."

Take the *japa-mālā* in the right hand, holding it between the thumb and the middle finger. The index finger is not used, as it is considered contaminated. Start at the bead next to the head bead. Before chanting Hare Kṛṣṇa *mahā-mantra japa*, chant the Pañca-tattva *mantra* : *śrī-kṛṣṇa-caitanya prabhu nityānanda / śrī-advaita gadādhara śrīvāsādi-gaura-bhakta-vṛnda.* Chanting these names of Lord Caitanya and His principal associates helps us become free from offences in chanting.

There are ten offences to be considered in chanting the holy names. These are described at the end of Chapter Eight of *The Nectar of Devotion*.

Now chant the *mahā-mantra*: Hare Kṛṣṇa, Hare Kṛṣṇa, Kṛṣṇa Kṛṣṇa, Hare Hare / Hare Rāma, Hare Rāma, Rāma Rāma, Hare Hare. Then move on to the second bead. In this way, after chanting the *mahā-mantra* fully each time, move to the next bead. After chanting 108 times, you will reach the head bead and will then have completed one *mālā*, or round. Now turn the beads around without crossing the head bead and start another round by again chanting *śrī-kṛṣṇa-caitanya prabhu nityānanda / śrī-advaita gadādhara śrīvāsādi-gaura-bhakta-vṛnda*.

Chanting is simple but should be performed properly for best results. Chant loudly enough so that at least someone sitting next to you can hear. While chanting, concentrate the mind on hearing the *mahā-mantra*. This concentration is *mantra* meditation and is powerful for cleaning our hearts. It is difficult to stop the mind from wandering, but, as with anything else, practice makes perfect. Note that the *mantra* should be chanted distinctly so that each syllable can be clearly heard.

Some devotees develop bad *japa* habits such as slurring or hissing the *mahā-mantra*, leaving out words or syllables, falling asleep while chanting, doing other things while chanting, intermittently talking with others, or reading while chanting. Another common mistake is skipping beads (unconsciously moving on to the next bead without fully finishing chanting one *mantra*,

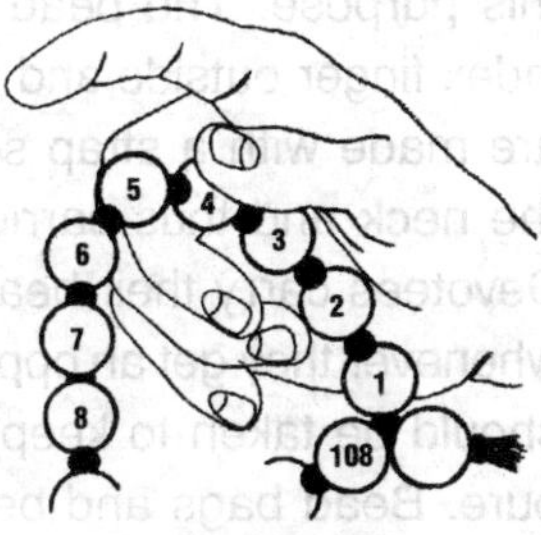

Holding Beads

thus chanting less than 108 times while going around). We have to constantly assess our *japa* performance to improve it.

Beginners in Kṛṣṇa consciousness have a tendency to take a long time chanting their rounds. However, practiced devotees usually finish sixteen rounds within one and a half to two hours (i.e., five and a half to eight minutes per round). Quality is more important than speed. So in the beginning concentrate on chanting clearly and hearing attentively. As one goes on chanting, speed usually develops automatically. If a round takes less than five minutes, it usually means that (a) the devotee is not concentrating properly, or (b) he is leaving out words or syllables of the *mantra*, or (c) he is skipping beads.

The best time to chant is early in the morning (during the *brāhma-muhūrta*, the auspicious period before sunrise). One can chant in any situation—on a train, while going to work, while walking on the street—but it is best to finish sixteen rounds with full concentration early in the morning, before starting our routine daily activities.

The *japa-mālā* is best kept in a special bag made for this purpose. The bead bag has a hole for keeping the index finger outside and away from the beads. Bead bags are made with a strap so that they may be worn around the neck and thus carried everywhere when not in use. Devotees carry their beads with them everywhere so that whenever they get an opportunity they can chant *japa*. Care should be taken to keep beads and bead bag clean and pure. Bead bags and beads are not taken into the toilet room.

Hearing from Advanced Devotees

nitya-siddha kṛṣṇa-prema 'sādhya' kabhu naya
śravaṇādi-śuddha-citte karaye udaya

"Pure love for Kṛṣṇa is eternally established in the hearts of the living entities. It is not something to be gained from another source. When the heart is purified by hearing and chanting, this love naturally awakens." (*Caitanya-caritāmṛta, Madhya-līlā* 22.107)

This is one of many scriptural verses emphasizing the importance of hearing about Kṛṣṇa from advanced devotees.

Those who live close to ISKCON centers can avail themselves of the opportunity to attend classes on *Śrīmad-Bhāgavatam* and *Bhagavad-gītā*, conducted every morning and evening.

In addition, devotees can listen to the several hundred recorded lectures of His Divine Grace A.C. Bhaktivedanta Swami Prabhupāda. There is no comparison to the

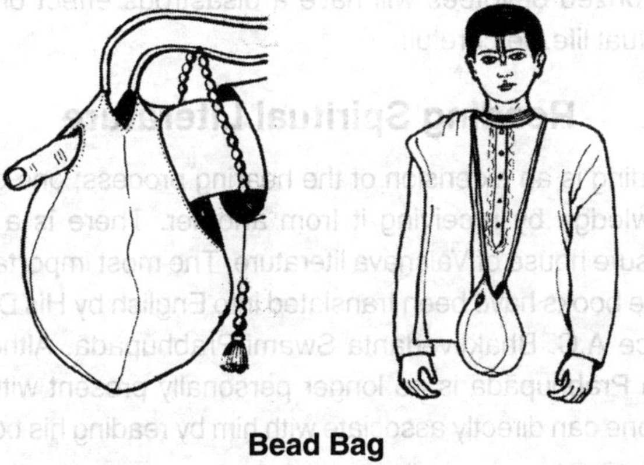

Bead Bag

transcendental sound vibration from the lips of a pure devotee of Kṛṣṇa.

Newcomers can approach senior devotees for personal consultation. Especially when first coming to Kṛṣṇa, we need a lot of help. For some it is difficult to adjust to different concepts and practices. Everyone has his own doubts and problems. So don't be shy about approaching mature devotees for guidance. That is what they are there for: to help others.

As much as hearing from bona fide devotees is purifying, hearing religious discourses from impersonalists, pseudodevotees, mundane scholars, professional lecturers, and other kinds of nondevotees is contaminating. The *Hari-bhakti-vilāsa* likens such discourses to milk touched by the lips of a serpent. Milk is delicious and nourishing, but if a snake drinks that milk, the remaining portion becomes poisonous. It may look and even taste the same, but is no longer beneficial: it's deadly. Similarly, lectures, dramas, and songs about Kṛṣṇa that are not performed by authorized devotees will have a disastrous effect on our spiritual life.Be careful!

Reading Spiritual Literature

Reading is an extension of the hearing process; one gains knowledge by receiving it from another. There is a vast treasure house of Vaiṣṇava literature. The most important of these books have been translated into English by His Divine Grace A.C. Bhaktivedanta Swami Prabhupāda. Although Śrīla Prabhupāda is no longer personally present with us, anyone can directly associate with him by reading his books.

Kṛṣṇa especially empowered Śrīla Prabhupāda to present all the subtleties of Vaiṣṇava understanding in straightforward English, just suitable for modern man to comprehend.

The easiest way to grasp the essence of Kṛṣṇa conscious philosophy is to read Śrīla Prabhupāda's books. Everything we need to know to become fully Kṛṣṇa conscious is completely described therein.

Prabhupāda stated that the most important of his books are *Bhagavad-gītā As It Is*, *Śrīmad-Bhāgavatam*, *Teachings of Lord Caitanya*, and *The Nectar of Devotion*. These are deeply philosophical works.

Beginners should start with introductory books such as *Civilization and Transcendence*; *Perfect Questions Perfect Answers*; *Kṛṣṇa, The Supreme Personality of Godhead*; and *The Science of Self-Realization*. *Message of Godhead* is invaluable for *gṛhasthas* because it describes how to live and work in this world as a *karma-yogī* and devotee. Another excellent book for beginners (or anyone else) is Śrīla Prabhupāda's biography, *Śrīla Prabhupāda Līlāmṛta*, by Satsvarūpa Dāsa Gosvāmī. Both the abridged and unabridged editions lucidly present Kṛṣṇa consciousness in the highly readable format of the story of a pure devotee.

When you feel ready to go on to the more difficult books, first read *Bhagavad-gītā As It Is*, *Śrī Īśopaniṣad*, *The Nectar of Instruction*, and *The Nectar of Devotion*. It is best to read *Bhagavad-gītā* through at least twice. Then go on to *Teachings of Lord Caitanya*, which Śrīla Prabhupāda called "our supermost contribution to the world."

Next go on to *Śrīmad-Bhāgavatam*. The *Bhāgavatam* is a multivolume work in twelve cantos. It is a great treasure house of devotion, transcendental knowledge, and Vedic culture — the spiritual encyclopaedia par excellence. Start from the beginning and read a little every day. In this way the whole *Bhāgavatam* may be read gradually. Next, go on to *Caitanya-caritāmṛta*, another multivolume work, which exhaustively and ecstatically describes the pastimes and philosophy of Lord Caitanya.

Even while studying *Śrīmad-Bhāgavatam* and other books, it is good to go on reading at least a little of the *Bhagavad-gītā* every day. There are also many other bona fide Vaiṣṇava books, but the most important books of Kṛṣṇa consciousness in the present age are those of Śrīla Prabhupāda.

Reading these Vaiṣṇava books on a daily basis is essential for all devotees. Read for one hour, two hours, or at least half an hour daily. As with all devotional activities, you should read with deep concentration and respect, praying to *guru* and Kṛṣṇa to bless you with the ability to understand such exalted subject matters. Those who develop a taste for transcendental literature will find their knowledge, wisdom, and love for Kṛṣṇa increasing every day. Such devotees can never be attracted to the garbage like books of mundane writers.

Association with Devotees

The scriptures repeatedly emphasize the importance of associating with devotees (*sādhu-saṅga*). It is considered the very root of devotion, being the cause of its sustenance and development. Caitanya Mahāprabhu said,

kṛṣṇa-bhakti-janma-mūla haya 'sādhu-saṅga'
kṛṣṇa-prema janme, teṅho punaḥ mukhya aṅga

"The root cause of devotional service to Lord Kṛṣṇa is association with devotees. Even when one's dormant love for Kṛṣṇa awakens, association with devotees is still most essential." (*Caitanya-caritāmṛta, Madhya-līlā* 22.83)

The two primary methods of associating with devotees are hearing from them and serving them. Devotees living in or adjacent to ISKCON centers can easily avail themselves of such opportunities. Always try to associate with devotees who are very serious about Kṛṣṇa consciousness.

Those living away from ISKCON centers can keep in touch by visiting them as often as possible. They can also correspond with devotees and take heart in the fact that by reading Śrīla Prabhupāda's books and serving his mission (especially by distributing his books) one is blessed with his association. It should be noted, however, that Śrīla Prabhupāda is always surrounded by his loving followers, so we should not neglect the association of his disciples and granddisciples presently available within ISKCON.

Maybe, unknown to you, there are people living near you who are interested in Kṛṣṇa. If so, the devotees at your nearest ISKCON center probably know them and could put you in touch with them. Then you could organize *kīrtana* meetings, festivals, and other activities together. If you distribute Śrīla Prabhupāda's books in your area, you are almost certain to eventually meet someone who will take a serious interest in Kṛṣṇa consciousness. So if you have no association, go out and find some!

In the Vedic tradition, householders invite *sannyasis* and saintly *brāhmaṇas* to their homes, feed them sumptuous *prasāda*, hear them and enquire from them, chant Hare Kṛṣṇa with them, serve them, and try to satisfy them in all respects. This is a form of *sādhu-saṅga* that is most pleasing and beneficial to all who participate.

The Four Regulative Principles

The four regulative principles of devotional service are as follows:

(1) No eating of meat, fish, or eggs.
(2) No intoxication.
(3) No gambling.
(4) No illicit sex life.

You must give up these four activities because they are the pillars of sinful life. They directly destroy the four pillars of religion: mercy, austerity, truthfulness, and cleanliness. If one is sinful and has no mercy, austerity, truthfulness, or cleanliness, how can he advance in spiritual life? Therefore strictly following these four regulative principles is a must for every devotee and, indeed, every civilized human being.

Apart from meat, fish, and eggs, garlic and onions are also forbidden for devotees. Factory-made bread and biscuits and other food cooked by nondevotees are also forbidden. Devotees like to take only *kṛṣṇa-prasāda*, food cooked specifically for the pleasure of the Lord and offered to Him with love and devotion.

Intoxicants include not only alcohol, *gāñjā*, and hard drugs but also tobacco, pan, betel nuts, betel powder, tea, coffee, and soft drinks containing caffeine (such as cola).

Chocolate also contains mild intoxicants and is therefore forbidden for devotees.

Along with gambling, all frivolous activities (watching TV, going to the cinema, mundane sports and music, etc.) are not meant for devotees. Note that lotteries are gambling.

Illicit sex means any sexual relationships other than those within marriage for the purpose of begetting Kṛṣṇa conscious children. Extramarital relationships are grossly sinful, spoil spiritual advancement, and therefore should not even be considered. Abortion, contraception, and sterilization are not only unnatural but also greatly sinful.

Masturbation is also illicit sex because it uselessly wastes vital fluid and contaminates our consciousness.

Modern so-called progressive civilization promotes sex so much that even those who are serious about spiritual advancement often find its attraction difficult to overcome. For help with this problem, it is best to have a frank talk with a devotee you deeply trust. Also, read *Brahmacarya in Kṛṣṇa Consciousness* (by the author of this book — available from the Bhaktivedanta Book Trust).

Setting Up a Temple at Home

It is essential for householder devotees (especially those who do not live near a temple community) to have a temple in their home. Having a temple at home and making it the center of family life transform an ordinary house into a sacred place.

Those with sufficient means and space sometimes construct a temple building separate from their house, but most devotees set aside a room in their residence as the temple room or *pūjā* room. Those with very limited space can simply set up an altar within their residential quarters.

The temple room is where the family members assemble for *kīrtana*, *ārati*, and readings from scripture; where offerings of food are made to Kṛṣṇa; and where the family members can come individually to chant *japa*, study the scriptures, and pray to Kṛṣṇa.

A separate room is much better than the "cupboard in the corner" set-up, because in a separate room an atmosphere of sanctity may be preserved. In other rooms the children can play and the adults can relax, socialize, and perform their household chores, but the temple room can be kept strictly for spiritual practices only.

The temple room is divided into the Deity room and the prayer hall. The Deity room is the section at the end of the temple room. It is separated from the prayer hall by a curtain. Even in situations where it is not possible to have a separate temple room, the Deities should be screened by a curtain.

In the household temple, the Lord and His pure devotees may be worshiped in their picture forms. Later, when the worshiping devotees become more advanced and experienced, they may install Deities. In fact, householder devotees who come up to the level of accepting initiation are expected to conduct Deity worship at home.

Advanced Deity worship should be undertaken under the guidance of a Vaiṣṇava *guru*; therefore, such worship has not been detailed in this book. If the worshiper actually has a spirit of devotion, worship of the Lord in His picture form is not inferior to the worship of the Lord in His Deity form, composed of wood, stone, or metal. But because such worship is a little detailed and complex, the facility for such worship is generally offered to devotees who have proved their dedication over a period of time.

A standard home altar should have the following pictures:

(1) The *sampradāya ācāryas*—(a) ISKCON Founder-*Ācārya*, A.C. Bhaktivedanta Swami Prabhupāda, (b) Bhaktisiddhānta Sarasvatī Ṭhākura, (c) Gaurakiśora Dāsa Bābājī, and (d) Bhaktivinoda Ṭhākura (Some devotees also keep a picture of Jagannātha Dāsa Bābājī, the *guru* of Bhaktivinoda Ṭhākura, on their altars.)

(2) The six Gosvāmīs of Vṛndāvana (Rūpa Gosvāmī, Sanātana Gosvāmī, Raghunātha Bhaṭṭa Gosvāmī,

Raghunātha Dāsa Gosvāmī, Gopāla Bhaṭṭa Gosvāmī, and Jīva Gosvāmī) were prominent disciples of Lord Caitanya who, under His direction, presented to the world the teachings and practices of Gauḍīya Vaiṣṇavism.

(3) The Pañca-tattva (Lord Caitanya and His four principal associates).

(4) Lord Nṛsiṁhadeva (devotees especially worship this form of the Lord because (a) He protects them from demons and disturbances — both prominent in this dark Age of Kali, and (b) He particularly helps the devotees uproot the demoniac desires from within their hearts).

(5) Rādhā-Kṛṣṇa.

(6) After taking initiation, or from the time one has formally accepted shelter of an ISKCON *guru* (See "The *Guru* and Initiation") a picture of one's *guru* is placed on the altar.

You should not place the pictures of those who are superior in the spiritual hierarchy below those who worship them. For example, never place the picture of the *guru* above that of Kṛṣṇa. The Pañca-tattva worship Rādhā-Kṛṣṇa and are worshiped by the *sampradāya ācāryas*. So the picture of the Pañca-tattva should be placed below that of Rādhā-Kṛṣṇa and above that of the *sampradāya ācāryas*.

In the pure Vaiṣṇava *sampradāya*, Kṛṣṇa, the original Personality of Godhead, is worshiped along with His expansions, internal energies, and pure devotee *ācāryas*. Lesser forms of worship, such as that of demigods, are not encouraged. Therefore Vaiṣṇavas are selective about which pictures they place on their altar. Although such respectable personalities as demigods and one's parents are certainly to be honored, they are not to be worshiped in the same place as Kṛṣṇa. As for pseudo-incarnations and bogus *sadhus*, they have no place at all.

The Deity room can be decorated tastefully, with flowers and garlands offered daily. Worship should be conducted as opulently as possible. Even those with little means should try to worship as well as possible, according to their capability. At least incense can be regularly burned and the temple room kept clean and tidy.

It is best to have an altar specially made from wood or other materials; it should be large enough so you can arrange all the pictures nicely on it. You should also keep a small table about three feet high, to hold the *ārati* plate, in front and to the left of the altar (on the left side of someone facing the altar). Another small table, about one foot high, is required for offering food, and a mat is also necessary. This mat should preferably be made of *kuśa* or other grass, or it can be cloth or wool. This is what you will sit on while performing *pūjā* or offering food.

There are many rules and regulations to be observed in the temple room, and these are listed in *The Nectar of Devotion*. Householders usually find it impossible to observe all the rules and regulations, but they should aim for as high a standard as is practical. The temple room is where we invite Kṛṣṇa, the master of multi-universes, to come in person and preside over our home; so we have to maintain a reverential attitude in the temple room.

Deity Worship, Pūjā, and Ārati

Here we can only briefly discuss this elaborate part of devotional service. The outline we give here will serve mostly as a guide for devotees living at home who have an altar with pictures, not installed Deities.

It is not necessary or even desirable for everyone to try to adopt complicated methods of worship. It is better to keep one's *pūjā* simple and concentrate more on the *yuga-dharma*, chanting the holy names of the Lord. Although eagerness to worship the Lord is certainly laudable, we should remember that the prime means of God realization in this age is chanting the holy names.[3] Therefore worship must be accompanied by *kīrtana* to be effective.

According to the *Hari-bhakti-vilāsa* and other authorized scriptures, different standards of worship are acceptable in different circumstances. The proper standard for Deity worship in the temple is to have regularly installed Deities worshiped strictly according to scriptural directions. But you may not be ready or capable of such worship. Therefore you may adjust your worship at home according to your capacity. It need not be like that in an opulent, well-established temple. It is for devotees worshiping at home that these directions are intended.

Another point is that there is no single, clearly-defined method of worship given in scripture. Therefore what we will give here are simple procedures that everyone can follow easily. For instance, at home it is quite acceptable and normal for women to perform *pūjā* and *āratis*, although it is unthinkable

[3] Devotees intersted in learning more about Deity worship can consult the official ISKCON guide.

that they could do so in the famous temples of India. Nevertheless, the generally accepted rule, even in homes, is that women do not engage in worship directly during the time of the month they are considered unclean.

Everything in the Deity room and all paraphernalia for worship should be kept spotlessly clean. The Deities Themselves, pictures, altar cloths, conches, cloths used in *ārati*, the floor and walls of the Deity room — all need regular cleaning. Deity dresses should be discarded and replaced at the first signs of becoming soiled and old. Brass and copper utensils should always be kept bright and shiny. Flowers used in worship are best removed from the altar at night.

Before offering *ārati* or performing *pūjā* (and even before cooking if worshiping installed Deities), one should bathe and put on fresh cloth. Silk is best for Deity worship. Cotton is also acceptable. Wool, although pure, is not worn in strict Deity worship. Polyester, terrycotton, and artificial cloth and cotton mixes are forbidden. Proper Vaiṣṇava dress should be worn (see "Vaiṣṇava Appearance"), not Western style outfit.

Although for householders some standards in Deity worship may be relaxed, devotees should not be miserly in their home worship. Unless completely poverty-stricken, one should at least use good-quality incense and flowers.

Kṛṣṇa belongs to the village atmosphere of Vṛndāvana and is thus greatly fond of flowers. He is more pleased with an offering of good flowers than with gold and jewels. Note that hibiscus (known as *jaba-phul* in Hindi), a red flower especially used in the worship of Lord Śiva and Durgā, is not preferred in the worship of Lord Viṣṇu and Vaiṣṇavas.

Offering Ārati

Place the following items on a plate specifically kept for this purpose (the "*ārati* plate"):

(1) A conch for blowing
(2) A cup filled with fresh water and holding a small spoon (*ācamana cup*).
(3) Incense — at least three sticks.
(4) *Pañcapradīpa* — a *ghee* lamp with five wicks (a ghee lamp with one wick may be used instead).
(5) A conch for offering water, and a stand to rest it on.
(6) A container of water for offering.
(7) A small piece of cloth. Handkerchiefs are commonly used. Varieties without printed writing on them are best. Two or three should be kept only for offering at *ārati*. The handkerchief must be clean and neatly folded.
(8) A small plate of flowers.
(9) An oil wick or candle (and matches).

Ārati Plate

(10) A *cāmara* (whisk).

(11) A peacock fan. (Items 10 and 11 should be permanently kept in the Deity room.)

Before offering *ārati*, pay obeisances outside the Deity room. Next, perform *ācamana* as follows. Take the spoon from the *ācamana* cup in your left hand, place water from the *ācamana* cup in your right hand, and then sip it. Then say *oṁ keśavāya namaḥ* and put another drop of water in your right hand. Repeat this procedure two times; the second time, after sipping water say *oṁ nārāyaṇāya namaḥ*, and the third time say *oṁ mādhavāya namaḥ*. You'll use the *ācamana* cup throughout the *ārati* to purify your hands and all objects offered. To purify an object, simply put three drops of water on it. Between offering items, purify your hand each time with three drops of water.

After performing *ācamana*, first purify the blowing conch (which is kept just outside the Deity room); take it in your right hand and blow three times. Purify it again, purify the right hand again, and enter the Deity room. From inside the Deity room open the curtains (which had hitherto been closed) while ringing the bell. (Upon seeing the Deities, all the devotees present in the temple room should bow down and offer obeisances; then they should stand up and begin *kīrtana*.)

Place the *ārati* plate on a small table, which is kept in the Deity room for that purpose. Now purify the incense (with three drops of water at the base) and light it. It's best to have an open oil lamp; next best is a candle. You should light either one with matches immediately upon entering the Deity room. Or you can keep an oil lamp permanently burning. In the rare case that neither a lamp nor candle is available, use matches to directly light the incense.

Purify both hands and the bell. Pick up the incense in the right hand and the bell in the left and start offering *ārati*, ringing the bell above the waist all the time while offering each item.

Pañcarātra-pradīpa, the ISKCON Deity worship book, recommends worshiping in the following manner. First, briefly show each item, beginning with the incense, to your *guru*, then to his *guru*, then to his *guru*, and so on, in this way showing each item to all the *paramparā gurus* whose pictures are on the alter. The idea is that you cannot offer anything directly to Kṛṣṇa, so first bring it to your *guru*, who brings it to his *guru*, who brings it to his *guru*, and so on. After thus taking permission from all your *gurus*, bring the item to Kṛṣṇa and worship Him by moving the item in clockwise circles, first offering to the feet, gradually rising up to the head, and then moving the item all around the body. Then worship Rādhā, then Lord Caitanya, then Lord Nityānanda, and finally the *paramparā gurus*, starting from the most senior and finishing with your own *guru*. The idea is that we worship Rādhā with that which has been offered to Kṛṣṇa, we worship Lord Caitanya with that which has been offered to Rādhā, and so on. Some systems of worship enjoin offering each item with a fixed number of circles. That is also good, but dedicating one's service to the Lord is more important than counting circles.

Offer *ārati* paraphernalia in the following order:

(1) Incense.
(2) Ghee Lamp.

(3) Water in a conch (this is a different conch from the one blown at the beginning of the *ārati*).
(4) A handkerchief or cloth.
(5) Flowers.
(6) *Cāmara*.
(7) Peacock fan (during the hot months).

When offering water in the conch, after offering water to each worshipable personality pour out three drops into a container kept for this purpose. After offering water to all the worshipable personalities, pour the balance left in the conch into the container. After offering the flowers, place one or more at the lotus feet of all the personalities you worshiped.

For offering the *cāmara* and fan, simply wave them a few times in the direction of each worshipable personality. In winter, when a cooling effect is undesirable, do not offer the fan. Remember to purify each item before offering it and to repurify your hand after offering each item.

You should complete the *ārati* in about twenty minutes, signalling its end by again blowing the conch three times. After purifying the conch with three drops of water, take the container with the water that was offered during *arati* and from the front of the Deity room sprinkle that water (from your right hand) over the heads of the assembled devotees. Next take some of the just-offered flowers from the altar and distribute them to the assembled devotees. Then remove the *ārati* paraphernalia for cleaning. (The devotees in the temple room should end the *kīrtana* and recite the *Jaya-dhvani* [see "Songs"].)

While performing *ārati*, concentrate on what you're doing — worshiping the Supreme Lord. Your attitude should be one of great awe and reverence.

Ārati is sometimes offered with only incense, flowers, and *cāmara*. This is called a *dhūpa-ārati*. But all the items mentioned above should be offered at *maṅgala-ārati* and *sandhyā-ārati*.

Pūjā

The scriptures describe many complex methods of *pūjā*. Here we will give only a basic outline, because doing complex *pūjā* is neither necessary nor possible for all. The proper system is to learn *pūjā* after receiving brahminical initiation, but this simplified outline is fine for beginners who want to do simple daily *pūjā* at home. These instructions are especially suitable for those worshiping pictures of the Lord. Devotees worshiping Deities of wood, metal, stone, or brass should consult an experienced *pūjārī*.

You should perform *pūjā* early in the morning, right after *maṅgala-ārati*. Before *pūjā* you should clean all the pictures, the altar, and the Deity room. The scriptures contain directions for worshiping with five, ten, sixteen, or sixty-four *upacāras* (items). The five items are *gandha* (scent), flowers, incense, a single ghee lamp, and *naivedya* (food).

First offer *pūjā* to your *guru*, then to Gaura-Nitāi, and then to Rādhā-Kṛṣṇa. After worshiping your *guru*, take permission from him (by praying to him) to worship Gaura-Nitāi and Rādhā-Kṛṣṇa. Worship with five items is conducted as follows.

Prepare *gandha*, a paste of sandalwood and camphor. (Use pink sandalwood, not the bright red variety.) Then, sitting on a mat on the Deity room floor, place the picture of your *guru* on a small table in front of you. Put a little *gandha* on the *guru's* forehead. Next, using the *gandha* paste affix a fresh Tulasī leaf to the *guru's* right hand. (Tulasī is offered only to the feet of Viṣṇu-tattva Deities. The idea behind placing Tulasī in the *guru's* hand is that he will place it at the lotus feet of Kṛṣṇa). Next, offer incense, a ghee lamp, and flowers (as in *ārati*). After offering the flowers, place them at the lotus feet of your *guru*. Next, place a fresh garland on the picture of your *guru* (either you or one of your family members can collect flowers and make garlands). Now do the *pūjā* in the same way for the Pañca-tattva, then for Rādhā-Kṛṣṇa. Now offer the *naivedya* (*bhoga* food preparations). You may offer either simple fruits, sweets, milk, etc., or cooked foods. Now the *pūjā* is finished and you should offer *ārati*.

Throughout the *pūjā*, chant and sing suitable *mantras* and songs in praise of your *guru*, Gaura-Nitāi, and Rādhā-Kṛṣṇa. In established temples the Deities' clothes are changed once or twice daily. But in home worship it is acceptable to change the Deities' clothes once a week.

Tulasī

"Tulasī is auspicious in all respects. Simply by seeing, simply by touching, simply by praying to, simply by bowing before, simply by hearing about, or simply by sowing this tree there is always auspiciousness. Anyone who comes in touch with the Tulasī tree in the above-mentioned ways lives eternally in the Vaikuṇṭha world." (*Skanda Purāṇa*)

Worship of the Tulasī plant is very important in devotional service. Tulasī is Kṛṣṇa's favorite plant, and He is very fond of her leaves and buds. Hence devotees should try to keep at least one or two Tulasī plants at home, water her daily, offer obeisances to her, and look after her carefully. Wherever Tulasī flourishes, *bhakti* also flourishes.

Tulasī ārati

In India, it is common to keep Tulasī on a plinth in one's courtyard and perform her daily *ārati* there. Those without such a facility should generally perform Tulasī *ārati* in the temple room. Before bringing Tulasī in, close the Deity room curtain, since Tulasī should not be worshiped in front of the Deities. As Tulasī is brought in, a devotee should chant the following *mantra* three times, and after each time all the devotees should chant responsively.

vṛndāyai tulasī-devyai
priyāyai keśavasya ca
viṣṇu-bhakti-prade devi
satyavatyai namo namaḥ

Place *Tulasī-devī* on a stand or table in the middle of the temple room. Then the song beginning with the words namo namaḥ *tulasī* should be sung (see "Songs") as the *ārati* is performed as follows:

The *ārati* plate should contain an *ācamana* cup, a bell, three sticks of incense, a ghee lamp, and a small plate of flowers. Matches or a lighted candle or oil lamp are also required. First perform *ācamana*. Then offer *Tulasī-devī* lighted incense, then the lighted ghee lamp, and then the flowers by waving the items in circles before her. After offering the incense, place it in an incense holder to continue burning. After offering the ghee lamp, hand it to another devotee, who should then take it to all the devotees present. They should place their hand first over the flame and then touch it to their heads. After offering the flowers, place a few at the base of Tulasī's stem and distribute the rest for the devotees to smell.

After the devotee singing the Tulasī song has finished it, he should sing the following *mantra* as the devotees all circumambulate Tulasī and water her with a few drops:

yāni kāni ca pāpāni
brahma-hatyādikāni ca
tāni tāni praṇaśyanti
pradakṣiṇaḥ pade pade

The *kīrtana* should end with several repetitions of the Hare Kṛṣṇa mantra.

A few more points about Tulasī

Tulasī leaves are essential for worshiping Viṣṇu. You should collect them in the morning (during daylight hours — not at night), using scissors reserved for this purpose. Be careful when circumambulating her and offering water to her, so that you do not hurt her in any way, Remember that Tulasī is not an ordinary plant; she is a great pure devotee.

Cut Tulasī's *mañjarīs* (seed receptacles, or buds) as soon as they appear. Otherwise many Tulasī plants will start to grow everywhere, and it will become difficult to care for them properly. Also, early cutting of *mañjarīs* helps Tulasī grow strong and healthy.

Keep Tulasī in such a way and in such a place that animals won't disturb her. (Dogs actually like to urinate on Tulasī, and goats like to eat her.) She should be placed away from pathways so that people will not thoughtlessly brush her as they pass. Children (and adults too!) should be trained to treat her respectfully. Tulasī does not like the hot summer sun, so try to keep her in the shade.

Although Tulasī has medicinal qualities, devotees do not think of her as medicine. She is a pure devotee and is worshipable by us. Devotees cultivate Tulasī to cultivate their devotion and for no other reason.

Tulasī leaves should be offered in devotion at the lotus feet of Viṣṇu-tattva Deities and pictures and to no one else. This means that Tulasī leaves are to be offered to the lotus feet of Lord Kṛṣṇa, Lord Nṛsiṁhadeva, Lord Caitanya, Nityānanda Prabhu, Advaita Prabhu, etc., but not to the lotus feet of even Rādhārāṇī, Gadādhara Paṇḍita, Śrīvāsa Paṇḍita, or the *sampradāya ācāryas*. However, in Deity worship you may place Tulasī in the right hand of your *guru* for him to offer at Kṛṣṇa's lotus feet. Tulasī leaves are also necessary for offering *bhoga* (food preparations) to the Lord.

The Daily Program

In all ISKCON temples, devotees gather in the mornings and evenings for a fixed program of spiritual practices. As much as possible, devotees living at home should bring their family members together for similar programs. Having a fixed daily program makes our Kṛṣṇa consciousness steady and strong.

Below is a typical daily schedule in an ISKCON temple. The schedule may vary slightly from temple to temple.

Morning Program

4.00 a.m. Devotees rise, shower, and put on *tilaka* and fresh clothes.

4.30 a.m.	*Maṅgala-ārati*
4.55 a.m.	*Jaya-dhvani* and Nṛsiṁha Prayers
5.00 a.m.	*Tulasī-ārati*
5.10 a.m.	*Japa* period begins. Most devotees chant *japa* at this time; the *pūjārīs* perform *pūjā* for the Deities and dress Them in fresh clothes.
7.00 a.m.	*Śṛṅgāra-ārati* (Greeting the Deities)
7.10 a.m.	*Guru-pūjā* (Worship of ISKCON Founder-*Ācārya* Śrīla Prabhupāda)
7.20 a.m.	*Śrīmad-Bhāgavatam* class
8.15 a.m.	(approximately) The morning program ends.

Evening Program

6.50 p.m.	*Tulasī-ārati*
7.00 p.m.	*Sandhyā-ārati*
7.25 p.m.	*Jaya-dhvani* and Nṛsiṁha Prayers
7.30 p.m.	*Bhagavad-gītā* class (about one hour).

Songs

The songs listed below are sung at specific times in all ISKCON centers throughout the world. Translations can be found in the book *Songs of the Vaiṣṇava Ācāryas*.

When To Sing	Song (opening words)
Maṅgala-ārati	*saṁsāra-dāvānala*
Tulasī-ārati	*namo namaḥ tulasī*
Guru-pūjā	*śrī-guru-caraṇa-padma*
Sandhyā-ārati	*jaya jaya gaurācānder*
Before class	*jaya rādhā-mādhava*

Before taking prasāda *śarīra abidyā-jāl*

After completing the songs at *maṅgala-ārati*, *tulasī-pūjā*, *guru-pūjā*, and *sandhyā-ārati*, continue the *kīrtana* with the Śrīla Prabhupāda *praṇāma-mantra*:

nama oṁ viṣṇu-pādāya kṛṣṇa-preṣṭhāya bhū-tale
śrīmate bhaktivedānta-svāminn iti nāmine
namas te sārasvate deve gaura-vāṇī-pracāriṇe
nirviśeṣa-śūnyavādi-pāścātya-deśa-tāriṇe

After this, continue the *kīrtana* with the Pañca-tattva mantra: *śrī-kṛṣṇa-caitanya prabhu nityānanda/śrī advaita gadādhara śrīvāsādi-gaura-bhakta-vṛnda.*

Sing this a few times (usually three), then continue with the *mahā-mantra*—Hare Kṛṣṇa, Hare Kṛṣṇa, Kṛṣṇa Kṛṣṇa, Hare Hare/Hare Rāma, Hare Rāma, Rāma Rāma, Hare Hare—until the end of the *ārati*.

After each *ārati*, the *Jaya-dhvani* is recited. Then the devotees sit and sing the song beginning with the words *namas te narasiṁhāya* (this is not sung after *guru-pūjā*).

Texts of songs

Śrī Śrī Gurv-aṣṭaka

saṁsāra-dāvānala-līḍha-loka-
trāṇāya kāruṇya ghanāghanatvam
prāptasya kalyāṇa-guṇārṇavasya
vande guroḥ śrī-caraṇāravindam

mahāprabhoḥ kīrtana-nṛtya-gīta-
vāditra-mādyan-manaso rasena
romāñca-kampāśru-taraṅga-bhājo
vande guroḥ śrī-caraṇāravindam

śrī-vigrahārādhana-nitya-nānā-
śṛṅgāra-tan-mandira-mārjanādau
yuktasya bhaktāṁś ca niyuñjato 'pi
vande guroḥ śrī-caraṇāravindam

catur-vidha-śrī-bhagavat-prasāda-
svādv-anna-tṛptān hari-bhakta-saṅghān
kṛtvaiva tṛptiṁ bhajataḥ sadaiva
vande guroḥ śrī-caraṇāravindam

śrī-rādhikā-mādhavayor apāra-
mādhurya-līlā-guṇa-rūpa-nāmnām
prati-kṣaṇāsvādana-lolupasya
vande guroḥ śrī-caraṇāravindam

nikuñja-yūno rati-keli-siddhyai
yā yālibhir yuktir apekṣaṇīyā
tatrāti-dākṣyād ati-vallabhasya
vande guroḥ śrī-caraṇāravindam

sākṣād-dharitvena samasta-śāstrair
uktas tathā bhāvyata eva sadbhiḥ
kintu prabhor yaḥ priya eva tasya
vande guroḥ śrī-caraṇāravindam

yasya prasādād bhagavat-prasādo
yasyāprasādān na gatiḥ kuto 'pi
dhyāyan stuvaṁs tasya yaśas tri-sandhyaṁ
vande guroḥ śrī-caraṇāravindam

Śrī Nṛsiṁha Praṇāma

namas te narasiṁhāya prahlādāhlāda-dāyine
hiraṇyakaśipor vakṣaḥ-śilā-ṭaṅka-nakhālaye

ito nṛsiṁhaḥ parato nṛsiṁho
yato yato yāmi tato nṛsiṁhaḥ
bahir nṛsiṁho hṛdaye nṛsiṁho
nṛsiṁham ādiṁ śaraṇaṁ prapadye

tava kara-kamala-vare nakham adbhuta-śṛṅgaṁ
dalita-hiraṇyakaśipu-tanu-bhṛṅgam
keśava dhṛta-narahari-rūpa jaya jagadīśa hare

Śrī Tulasī-kīrtana

namo namaḥ tulasī! kṛṣṇa-preyasī
rādhā-kṛṣṇa-sevā pābo ei abhilāṣī

je tomāra śaraṇa loy, tara vāñchā pūrṇa hoy
kṛpā kori' koro tāre bṛndāvana-bāsī

mor ei abhilāṣ, bilās kuñje dio vās
nayane heribo sadā jugala-rūpa rāśi

ei nivedana dharo, sakhīr anugata koro
sevā-adhikāra diye koro nija dāsī

dīna kṛṣṇa-dāse koy, ei jena mora hoy
śrī-rādhā-govinda-preme sadā jena bhāsi

Śrī Guru-vandanā

śrī-guru-caraṇa-padma, kevala-bhakati-sadma,
bandõ mui sāvadhāna mate

jāhāra prasāde bhāi, e bhava toriyā jāi,
kṛṣṇa-prāpti hoy jāhā ha 'te

guru-mukha-padma-vākya, cittete koriyā aikya,
ār nā koriho mane āśā

śrī-guru-caraṇe rati, ei se uttama-gati,
je prasāde pūre sarva āśā

cakhu-dān dilo jei, janme janme prabhu sei,
divya-jñān hṛde prokāśito

prema-bhakti jāhā hoite, avidyā vināśa jāte,
vede gāy jāhāra carito

śrī-guru karuṇā-sindhu, adhama janāra bandhu,
lokanāth lokera jīvana

hā hā prabhu koro doyā, deho more pada-chāyā,
ebe jaśa ghuṣuk tribhuvana

Jaya Rādhā-Mādhava

(jaya) rādhā-mādhava kuñja-bihārī
gopī-jana-vallabha giri-vara-dhārī

jaśodā-nandana, braja-jana-rañjana
jāmuna-tīra-vana-cārī

Prasāda-sevāya

śarīra abidyā-jāl, joḍendriya tāhe kāl,
jīve phele viṣaya-sāgore

tā'ra madhye jihwāti, lobhamoy sudurmati,
tā'ke jetā kaṭhina saṁsāre

kṛṣṇa baro doyāmoy, koribāre jihwā jay,
swa-prasād-anna dilo bhāi

sei annāmṛta pāo, rādhā-kṛṣṇa-guṇa gāo,
preme ḍako caitanya-nitāi

Gaura-ārati

jaya jaya gorācānder āratiko śobhā
jāhnavī-taṭa-vane jaga-mana-lobhā

Refrain (1) *gaurāṅger ārotik śobhā*
jaga-jana-mana-lobhā

dakhiṇe nitāicānd, bāme gadādhara
nikaṭe adwaita, śrīnivāsa chatra-dhara

bosiyāche gorācānd ratna-siṁhāsane
ārati koren brahmā-ādi deva-gaṇe

narahari-ādi kori' cāmara dhulāya
sañjaya-mukunda-bāsu-ghoṣ-ādi gāya

śaṅkha bāje ghaṇṭā bāje bāje karatāla
madhura mṛdaṅga bāje parama rasāla

Refrain (2) śankha bāje ghaṇṭā bāje
madhur madhur madhur bāje

bahu-koti candra jini' vadana ujjvala
gala-deśe bana-mālā kore jhalamala

śiva-śuka-nārada preme gada-gada
bhakativinoda dekhe gorāra sampada

Jaya-dhvani

Jaya oṁ viṣṇu-pāda paramahaṁsa parivrājakācārya
aṣṭottara-śata śrī śrīmad abhaya caraṇāravinda
A.C. bhaktivedānta svāmī mahārāja prabhupāda kī jaya!
Jaya oṁ viṣṇupāda paramahaṁsa parivrājakācārya
aṣṭottara śata śrī śrīmad bhaktisiddhānta sarasvatī
gosvāmī mahārāja prabhupāda ṭhākura kī jaya!

ananta koṭi vaiṣṇava-vṛnda kī jaya!
nāmācārya śrīla haridāsa ṭhākura kī jaya!

prem-se kaho śrī-kṛṣṇa-caitanya prabhu nityananda śrī-
advaita gadādhara śrīvāsādi-gaura-bhakta-vṛnda kī jaya!

śrī-śrī rādhā-kṛṣṇa gopa-gopīnātha śyāma-kuṇḍa
rādhā-kuṇḍa giri-govardhana kī jaya!

vṛndāvana-dhāma kī jaya!
navadvīpa-dhāma kī jaya!
mathurā-dhāma kī jaya!
dvārakā-dhāma kī jaya!
jagannātha-purī dhāma kī jaya!
gaṅgā-mayī kī jaya!
yamunā-mayī kī jaya!

bhakti-devī kī jaya!
tulasī-devī kī jaya!
samāveta bhakta-vṛnda kī jaya!
gaura-premānande hari, haribol!

All glories to the assembled devotees — Hare Kṛṣṇa!
All glories to the assembled devotees — Hare Kṛṣṇa!
All glories to the assembled devotees — Hare Kṛṣṇa!
All glories to Śrī Guru and Śrī Gaurāṅga!

(All the devotees audibly recite the *guru-praṇāma* mantra.)

Kṛṣṇa Prasāda

The preparation, offering, and distribution of ***prasāda*** (food offered to Viṣṇu) form a major part of Vaiṣṇava culture. Nondevotees cannot understand how Kṛṣṇa eats, because the food appears to remain untouched. But factually He does eat, and devotees take the vow to eat only the remnants of what He has eaten.

Preparation

Kṛṣṇa eats only food offered with love and devotion. Therefore procure good-quality fruits, vegetables, sugar, grains, and milk products, and with care and attention prepare tasty dishes from these ingredients for Kṛṣṇa's pleasure.

Meat, fish, eggs, garlic, onions, mushrooms, vinegar, and masur (red) dhal cannot be offered to Kṛṣṇa Excessively spicy foods are also unfit for offering.

Milk should preferably be cow's milk. Ghee (specifically cow-milk ghee) is best for cooking for Kṛṣṇa. If you cannot procure it, use oil. Traditionally acceptable oils are mustard oil and sesame oil. Due to the high price of first-class ingredients in the modern age, many devotees living at home, worshiping Kṛṣṇa according to their means, cook with other oils, such as groundnut oil.

While cooking, think of how Kṛṣṇa will enjoy the offering rather than of your own enjoyment. Take care that you prepare the offering cleanly. No one, including the cook, can taste the food until after it has been offered to Kṛṣṇa.

Offering

Keep a special plate and glass exclusively for offering food to Kṛṣṇa. Place food prepared for Him on the plate, along with a glass of fresh drinking water. You can also place lemon slices on the plate (cut the lemon in quarters and remove the seeds), along with a little salt. You can place liquid items (such as dhal) in small dishes (*katories*) kept only for these offerings. On each preparation place a Tulasī leaf.

When the plate is all arranged, place it on either the altar or a table in front of the altar, or (if there is no altar arrangement) in front of a picture of Kṛṣṇa. As you sit in front of the altar and meditate on how Kṛṣṇa will enjoy the offering, ring the bell while reciting each of the following prayers three times:

(1) *nama oṁ viṣṇu-pādāya kṛṣṇa-preṣṭhāya bhū-tale*
śrīmate bhaktivedānta-svāminniti nāmine
namas te sārasvate deve gaura-vāṇī-pracāriṇe
nirviśeṣa-śūnyavādi-pāścātya-deśa-tāriṇe

(2) *namo mahā-vadānyāya kṛṣṇa-prema-pradāya te*
kṛṣṇāya kṛṣṇa-caitanya-nāmne gaura-tviṣe namaḥ

(3) *namo brahmaṇya-devāya go-brāhmaṇa-*
hitāya ca jagad-dhitāya kṛṣṇāya govindāya namo namaḥ

From the time you take formal shelter of an ISKCON *guru* (see "The *Guru* and Initiation"), you should recite the *mantra* of your own *guru* three times before reciting Śrīla Prabhupāda's *praṇāma mantra* (the first in the list above).

Meditate on offering the food to your *guru*, who then offers it to Kṛṣṇa. Leave the offering in front of Kṛṣṇa for fifteen minutes. Then remove the plate and transfer the items from it, either back to the pots in which they were cooked or onto a plate kept only for distributing *mahā-prasāda*.

This system of offering, although simple, is acceptable to Kṛṣṇa if everything is offered with love.

Terminology

Uncooked or unoffered food is called *bhoga*. Prepared food ready to be offered is also called *bhoga*, or more precisely *naivedya*. Food that has been offered to Kṛṣṇa is called *prasāda* or *mahā-prasāda*. And remnants of *prasāda* left by a pure devotee are called *mahā-mahā-prasāda*.

Cooking and Eating Utensils

Aluminium pots are poisonous and therefore unsuitable to use in cooking for Kṛṣṇa.

Ceramic, glass, aluminum, and plastic plates and cups are considered low class in Vedic culture. Eating utensils made of silver, stone, and brass are all acceptable.

Stainless steel, traditionally considered impure, has also become widely accepted in many high-class homes. Best of all are plates made of leaves, which are used once and then thrown away.

HONORING PRASĀDA

Taking *prasāda* is not like eating ordinary food. Therefore we speak of "honoring" or "serving," not "eating," *prasāda*. Taking *kṛṣṇa-prasāda* is a great privilege. The remnants of food offered to Kṛṣṇa are called *prasāda* ("Kṛṣṇa's mercy") because Kṛṣṇa is so kind that He helps us make spiritual advancement even by eating. *Kṛṣṇa-prasāda* is nondifferent from Kṛṣṇa and should therefore be served and honored with awe and reverence.

Before taking *prasāda*, chant the prayer beginning with the words *śarīra abidyā-jāl*.

Devotees sit to honor *prasāda*. Standing while eating is not only uncultured but also unhealthy. Devotees should eat all that is put onto their plates. To throw away even ordinary food is sinful, what to speak of *kṛṣṇa-prasāda*. Therefore servers should serve a little at a time. In Vedic culture the left hand is not used for eating; only the right hand is used. *Prasāda* is best honored in a peaceful, happy, and relaxed mood.

Food and Eating Habits

The Vedic literature states, *āhāra-śuddhau sattva-śuddhiḥ*: "If one's food is pure, one's whole existence is pure."

Traditionally the followers of Vedic culture were strict about what they ate. The reason is that the consciousness of the cook enters the food. Devotees who eat food cooked by persons of unclean habits and impure consciousness become contaminated by the mentality of the cook and share in their sinful karmic reactions. As Lord Caitanya said, "When one eats food cooked by a materialistic person, one's mind becomes contaminated. When the mind becomes contaminated, one is unable to think of Kṛṣṇa properly." (*Śrī Caitanya-caritāmṛta, Antya-līlā* 6.278) Therefore devotees practice taking only *kṛṣṇa-prasāda*.

Prasāda is not only karma-free but also purifying. This is because it is cooked and offered to Kṛṣṇa with love by devotees following the principles of Kṛṣṇa consciousness. Strictness in eating is required for rapid advancement in Kṛṣṇa consciousness. The best thing is to arrange life so as to eat only kṛṣṇa-prasāda.

However, this is not always possible for all devotees. A busy working single person, or someone who travels a lot, may sometimes have to purchase food to eat. If buying food outside, it is best to buy fruit. Milk products (milk, yogurt, milk sweets, cheese, etc.) are also considered pure even if prepared by nondevotees.

For devotees, eating in *karmī*[4] restaurants is not good. In unusual circumstances, if you feel constrained to do so, you should select a clean vegetarian restaurant. Check that the preparations are free of onions and garlic. Never eat even vegetarian food in a restaurant that also serves meat.

Currently there is widespread propaganda in India that eggs are vegetarian food. From the biological standpoint, fertilized eggs are embryos (liquid flesh). Unfertilized eggs are the menstruation of chickens. *Śāstra* clearly declares

[4] One who is engaged in karma (fruitive activity); a materialist

eggs to be nonvegetarian food. Any propaganda to the contrary is simply bogus. Never mind what ill-motivated scientists, politicians, and eggsellers would have us believe.

By the law of *karma*, grains cooked by nondevotees are especially contaminated by karmic reactions. Occasionally taking puffed rice, popcorn, etc., cooked by nondevotees, though not very good, is not very harmful either. But *karmī* bread and biscuits should be completely avoided, as they have a heavy karmic influence.

Onions and garlic are strictly forbidden for devotees. They are not offerable to Kṛṣṇa. Like meat, they adversely affect the consciousness with the lowest mode of nature (*tamo-guṇa*, the mode of ignorance).

You should even give up mild intoxicants like tea, coffee, and chocolate because they are unhealthy, unclean, unnecessary, habit-forming, and unofferable to Kṛṣṇa.

Also, be careful about nonvegetarian ingredients in food cooked by nondevotees. Bread, biscuits, ice cream, canned foods (and in the Western countries cheese and yogurt) often contain egg derivatives, rennet (made from the lining of cows' stomachs), or gelatin (extracted from animal bones). Sometimes the list of ingredients on the package may include "shortening," "lecithin," or some mysterious chemical. These may or may not be vegetarian. In such a case, better to be safe than sorry. Don't buy it.

On the whole, somehow or other sticking to the principle of taking only *kṛṣṇa-prasāda* is the best. Today people are often too lazy to cook, but even for physical health home-cooked food is best — and what to speak of spiritual health.

Tilaka

Wearing *tilaka* is essential for all devotees. *Tilaka* is for both purification and protection. Furthermore, it is a beautiful decoration that clearly declares to the world that the wearer is a devotee of Viṣṇu. When people see devotees wearing *tilaka*, they are reminded of Kṛṣṇa and thus purified.

Sadly, some devotees, fearing ridicule, feel shy about wearing *tilaka*. But those who boldly wear *tilaka* at all times — even in their workplace — soon find the ridicule replaced with respect. If you feel you can't wear *tilaka* publicly, at least apply "water *tilaka*." Instead of applying *gopīcandana* paste, make invisible *tilaka* marks with water and say the appropriate *mantras*. That way, at least you'll be protected by the *mantras*. The scripture allows various kinds of substances to be used for applying *tilaka*. Most Gauḍīya Vaiṣṇavas use *gopīcandana* — a yellow clay sold in Vṛndāvana and Navadvīpa and also available at most ISKCON centers. *Tilaka* is generally applied after bathing. In this way a Vaiṣṇava wears *tilaka* at all times, not just at the time of *pūjā*. To apply *tilaka*, put a little water in the palm of your left hand. Then take a piece of *gopīcandana* in your right hand and rub it in the water to make a smooth paste.

Take some of the *gopīcandana* mixture in your left palm onto the end of the ring finger of the right hand. Then apply this *tilaka*, first to the forehead. Press firmly to make two vertical lines. The movement should be from the top of the nose upwards (not downwards) and may be repeated several times to get the correct design: two straight, neat, parallel lines. Then apply the *gopīcandana* paste on the nose with a downward motion. The correct length is three-

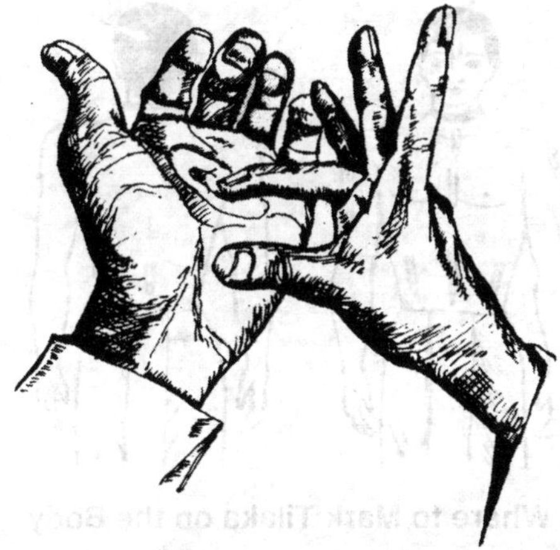

Applying Tilaka

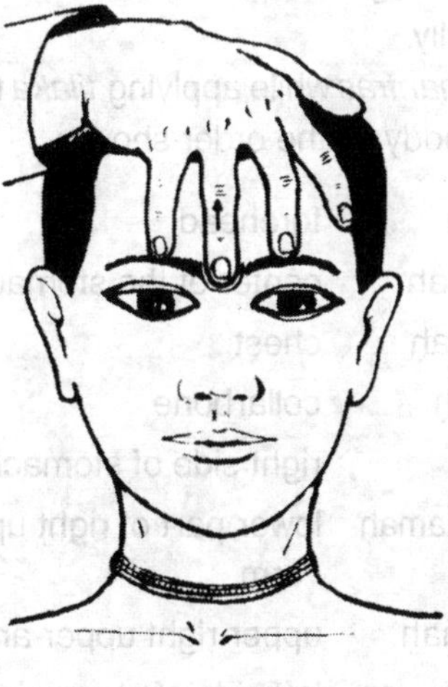

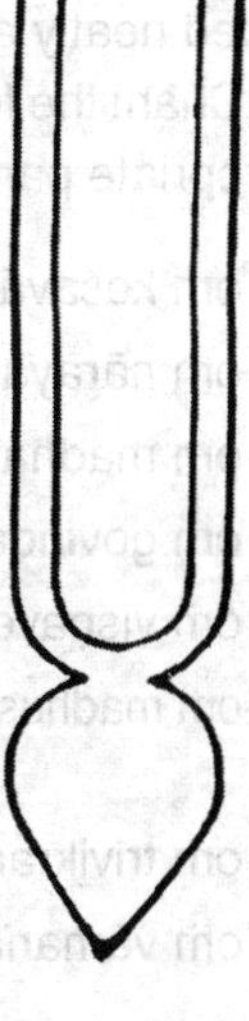

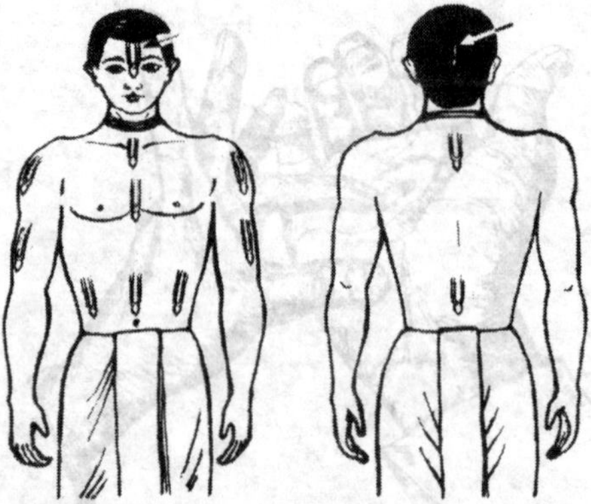

Where to Mark Tilaka on the Body

quarters the length of the nose(i.e., not very short but not the full length of the nose). Join the marks on the forehead and nose at the bridge of the nose, leaving no gap between them. Look in the mirror to get it right. *Tilaka* should be applied neatly and carefully.

Chant the following *mantras* while applying *tilaka* to the appropriate parts of the body, in the order shown:

(1)	oṁ keśavāya namaḥ	forehead
(2)	oṁ nārāyaṇāya namaḥ	center of the stomach
(3)	oṁ mādhavāya namaḥ	chest
(4)	oṁ govindāya namaḥ	collarbone
(5)	oṁ viṣṇave namaḥ	right side of stomach
(6)	oṁ madhusūdanāya namaḥ	lower part of right upper arm
(7)	oṁ trivikramāya namaḥ	upper right upper arm
(8)	oṁ vāmanāya namaḥ	left side of stomach

(9)	oṁ śrīdharāya namaḥ	lower part of left upper arm
(10)	oṁ hṛṣīkeśāya namaḥ	upper part of left upper arm
(11)	oṁ padmanābhāya namaḥ	upper back
(12)	oṁ dāmodarāya namaḥ	lower back
(13)	oṁ vāsudevāya namaḥ	top of head

Apply *tilaka* with the fourth finger of your right hand. Apply the two marks on the right arm with the fourth finger of your left hand. After applying *tilaka*, smear whatever little *gopīcandana* paste remains in your left palm on the top of your head, in the area just above the *śikhā*.

Care of Sacred Items

Sacred items (such as spiritual books, *pūjā* paraphernalia, beads and bead bags, *mṛdaṅgas*, *karatālas*, and pictures of the Supreme Lord or His devotees), should all be kept carefully and respectfully. Keep them neatly and never put them in a contaminated place or near unclean things. After using them, put them away tidily; do not simply leave them strewn here and there. They should never be put on the floor or stepped over.

Cleanliness

In the *Bhagavad-gītā* Lord Kṛṣṇa mentions cleanliness as a divine quality and as the symptom of a *brāhmaṇa*. He declares uncleanliness to be a symptom of the demoniac. Caitanya Mahāprabhu listed cleanliness as one of the twenty-six qualities of a devotee. And Śrīla Prabhupāda was so insistent that his disciples observe the rules of cleanliness that he would severely chastise devotees who were negligent in this regard.

The rules of cleanliness form an elaborate part of Vedic culture, and to expound on them in detail is beyond the scope of this book. But cleanliness is essential for all devotees. The main way to attain internal cleanliness is to chant the *mahā-mantra:*

Hare Kṛṣṇa, Hare Kṛṣṇa,
Kṛṣṇa Kṛṣṇa, Hare Hare
Hare Rāma, Hare Rāma,
Rāma Rāma, Hare Hare

Externally, a devotee keeps his body, clothes, possessions, residence, and everything else always neat, clean, and tidy. Devotees wear freshly washed clothes every day and take a bath or shower at least once a day.

ISKCON

ISKCON (The International Society for Krishna Consciousness) was founded in New York in 1966 by His Divine Grace A.C. Bhaktivedanta Swami Prabhupāda. It rapidly expanded to become a worldwide confederation of several hundred temples and ashrams with affiliated farm communities and *gurukula* schools.

ISKCON is based on the timeless teachings of the *Bhagavad-gītā* and *Śrīmad-Bhāgavatam*, as received in disciplic succession from Lord Caitanya Mahāprabhu. Lord Caitanya appeared in 1486 in Māyāpur Dhāma and taught the science of *kṛṣṇa-bhakti*. He popularized the chanting of Hare Kṛṣṇa, Hare Kṛṣṇa, Kṛṣṇa Kṛṣṇa, Hare Hare / Hare Rāma, Hare Rāma, Rāma Rāma, Hare Hare, the *mahā-*

mantra ("great chanting for deliverance"), which is most effective in this Age of Kali. ISKCON is meant to fulfill Lord Caitanya's mission by preaching Kṛṣṇa consciousness all over the world.

ISKCON is part of the Gauḍīya Vaiṣṇava *sampradāya*. One can trace its spiritual lineage from Śrīla Prabhupāda back through a chain of spiritual masters, through Lord Caitanya, through Madhvācārya, to Lord Brahmā, and ultimately to Lord Kṛṣṇa Himself. This principle of *paramparā* (unbroken disciplic succession) is a major hallmark of ISKCON's authenticity.

Śrīla Prabhupāda set up ISKCON so that all persons who join this society can get everything they need to achieve all perfection in Kṛṣṇa consciousness.

Managerially, ISKCON is divided into zones — about thirty at present, comprising the whole world. Each zone is overseen by at least one senior devotee known as a Governing Body Commissioner (GBC Officer). Some zones have two or more co-GBCs. The highest managerial authority in ISKCON is the GBC body (composed of all GBC officers). The GBC body meets once yearly in Māyāpur to review and plan the activities of the society. Decisions within the GBC body are made by voting.

Within each GBC zone are several temples. Each temple is independent, both financially and, to a large extent, managerially. Thus, there is no single head office of ISKCON, although Māyāpur is considered the spiritual world headquarters. Each temple has a Temple President, who is its main managing officer and temporal authority. The GBC Officer regularly visits the temples in his zone to help ensure that the spiritual standards are being maintained, to see that management and development are going on nicely, and to co-ordinate preaching within the zone.

Śrīla Prabhupāda said that the GBC officers should be like watchdogs. This means that they always have to be alert for the well-being of ISKCON, and especially to prevent philosophical contaminations from entering and polluting the society.

Śrīla Prabhupāda also said that "leader means leader in hearing and chanting." Therefore leaders in ISKCON should not only manage and organize but also uphold ideal standards of spiritual practice and behavior. Śrīla Prabhupāda stressed that high spiritual standards could best be maintained in ISKCON if the leaders set an exemplary standard in hearing and chanting.

Unlike when Śrīla Prabhupāda was physically present, there is now no single leader of ISKCON. Śrīla Prabhupāda himself said that all his disciples — those who followed — would become leaders in his physical absence. He instructed his disciples to work co-operatively to help spread Kṛṣṇa consciousness, and this order remains the key to the continuing spread of the movement.

Preaching

In the *Bhagavad-gītā* (18.69) Lord Kṛṣṇa states that no one in this world is more dear to Him than one who preaches His message. And Śrīla Prabhupāda writes (*Śrīmad-Bhāgavatam* 7.6.24 purport): "Preaching is the easiest way to realize the Supreme Personality of Godhead."

Lord Caitanya instructed, "Whomever you meet, tell them about Kṛṣṇa. In this way, on My order, become a *guru* and deliver this land." (*Śrī Caitanya-caritāmṛta, Madhya-līlā* 7.128). So, on Lord Caitanya's order, devotees should not be content simply to perform devotional activities for their own upliftment but must try to give Kṛṣṇa consciousness to others.

Everybody can preach. Even if a devotee is not very learned in Vaiṣṇava philosophy, he can still request everyone he meets to chant Hare Kṛṣṇa. However, it is essential that those who are active in preaching work thoroughly and regularly study Śrīla Prabhupāda's books.

The best way to preach is to distribute Śrīla Prabhupāda's books. We may be able to speak to someone for a few minutes, but if they take a book they can study it for several hours, keep it at home, or give it to someone else. Prabhupāda's books give a clear, straightforward presentation of the philosophy of Kṛṣṇa consciousness directly from the topmost empowered devotee. And one book may be read by many people. Therefore, Śrīla Prabhupāda certified that book distribution is the best preaching.

> There is no comparison, there is no literature, throughout the whole universe like *Śrīmad-Bhāgavatam*. There is no comparison, there is no competition. Every word is for the good of the human society. Every word, each and every word. Therefore we are stressing so much on the book distribution. Somehow or other, if the book goes in one's hand, he'll be benefited. At least he'll see, 'They've taken so much

> price, let me see what is there.' If he reads one *śloka* his life will be successful. If he reads one *śloka*...one word. It is such a nice thing. Therefore we are stressing so much, 'Please distribute books, distribute books, distribute books.'
>
> [Śrīla Prabhupāda]

To get more information and inspiration about preaching, read *Preaching Is the Essence* by Śrīla Prabhupāda (available from the Bhaktivedanta Book Trust).

Nagara-Saṅkīrtana

When a group of devotees goes on the streets of a town or village and loudly sings the holy names of the Lord to the accompaniment of *mṛdaṅgas* and *karatālas*, that is called *nagara-saṅkīrtana*. Lord Caitanya Mahāprabhu, who is Kṛṣṇa Himself, the Supreme Personality of Godhead, personally propagated *saṅkīrtana*. *Saṅkīrtana* takes the mercy of Kṛṣṇa's holy names to the spiritually dull mass of people and, indeed, to all living entities, who would otherwise have no exposure to Kṛṣṇa consciousness.

Public chanting purifies the contaminated atmosphere of Kali-yuga, and anyone who takes part in it becomes dear to Lord Caitanya. The more devotees that join the *saṅkīrtana* party, the better. But if many devotees are not available, even three or four devotees can go out, or even two — even one. Distribution of Śrīla Prabhupāda's books and *kṛṣṇa-prasāda* make the *saṅkīrtana* party even more transcendentally enlivening. If you use a megaphone, more conditioned living entities will benefit from hearing the holy name. You can also take out colorful banners and flags to enhance the festive mood.

Go on *harināma-saṅkīrtana* as often as possible, for as long as possible, and just see how Lord Caitanya blesses you!

Ekādaśī

Ekādaśī is a day of fasting that all devotees observe. Failure to do so is a serious offence. There are two Ekādaśīs every month: on the eleventh day after the new moon, and on the eleventh day after the full moon. Ekādaśī literally means "the eleventh day."

Śrīla Prabhupāda usually observed the Ekādaśī fast in the simplest manner prescribed in scripture: by refraining from eating grains, beans, peas, and dahl. Some devotees eat only fruit on Ekādaśī, some take only water, and some fully fast(this is called *nirjala-vrata*, literally "the vow of not taking even water").

Devotees must avoid the following foods on Ekādaśī: all grains (wheat, rice, etc.), dahl, peas, vegetables in the bean family, and mustard seeds, along with foods that are derivatives of these items (wheat flour, mustard oil, soya-bean oil, etc.) and foods containing these products (for instance, we should be careful to avoid using any powdered spices that are mixed with flour).

One should break the Ekādaśī fast the next day (Dvādaśī) by taking *prasāda* prepared with grains. The fast must be broken within a specific interval (between 5:00 a.m. and 9:00 a.m., for example). For the dates of Ekādaśīs and the times for breaking fasts, consult the Vaiṣṇava calendar, which is available from any ISKCON center. One should be careful to consult only the calendar used by ISKCON, since dates for Ekādaśī and other important festivals may vary according to the system of calculation used by pandits in other *sampradāyas*. The real purpose of observing Ekādaśī is, however, not simply to fast but to increase the time we spend hearing and chanting about Kṛṣṇa. Śrīla Prabhupāda recommended that devotees with sufficient time chant twenty-five or more rounds of *japa* on Ekādaśī.

Shaving and cutting of one's nails is also forbidden on Ekādaśī.

Cāturmāsya and Dāmodara Vrata

Cāturmāsya is a four-month period of austerity observed during the rainy season. Traditionally, during the monsoon those sadhus and sannyasis who travel from place to place to enlighten the general populace stop their wanderings and remain in a holy place for four months to worship the Lord with vows of austerity.

However, members of ISKCON, on the order of Śrīla Prabhupāda, do not stop their intensive preaching activities during the rainy season and therefore do not observe severe Cāturmāsya vows. They may observe the following dietary restrictions: During the first month they do not eat cooked green leafy vegetables, during the second month, yogurt, during the third month, milk, and during the fourth month, urad dahl.

Devotees observe the Cāturmāsya period during the four months of the rainy season in India (approximately

July through October). Cāturmāsya extends from Śayana Ekādaśī (in the month of Āṣāḍha) to Uttara Ekādaśī (in the month of Kārtika), or from Āṣāḍha Pūrṇimā to Kārtika Pūrṇimā, or simply from the start of the month of Śravaṇa to the end of Kārtika (consult the Vaiṣṇava calendar for the exact dates).

The fourth month of Cāturmāsya, Kārtika, is dedicated to Lord Kṛṣṇa in His Dāmodara form and is known as Dāmodara month. The name Dāmodara (literally "He with a rope [*dāma*] around His belly [*udara*]) refers to a pastime of Kṛṣṇa's in which His mother, Yaśodā, tied Him up with a rope around His belly to punish Him for some mischief."

During Kārtika, many Vaiṣṇavas go to Vṛndāvana and reside there for the whole month, following special vows. In the temples, a picture of Dāmodara and Yaśodā is placed on the altar, and morning and evening all devotees individually offer ghee lamps to the Deities (from outside the Deity room) while congregationally singing the *Dāmodarāṣṭaka* (see *Songs of the Vaiṣṇava Ācāryas*).

Festivals

Every day in Kṛṣṇa consciousness is a festival. Singing and dancing in saintly company, relishing the beauty of the Deity, devotees daily celebrate the bliss of serving Kṛṣṇa. Still, devotees observe special festivals on the appearance days of the Lord, His incarnations, and His great devotees, as well as on those days commemorating His special *līlās* (pastimes).

Festivals revive and nourish our *bhakti* and are thus considered the mother of devotion. They are joyous occasions for devotees to come together and glorify Kṛṣṇa. Devotees who, for whatever reason, cannot regularly visit ISKCON centers often make it a point to attend on festival days. Devotees living at home, far from an ISKCON center, can arrange a festival according to their means and invite their neighbors to share the bliss of Kṛṣṇa consciousness.

To celebrate a festival, devotees decorate the temple room and cook large quantities of sumptuous food, which they offer to Kṛṣṇa and distribute liberally. Continuous hearing and chanting of the glories of Kṛṣṇa and His devotees surcharge the atmosphere with spiritual sound.

Festival days are especially suitable for performing devotional dramas and going out on *nagara saṅkīrtana*. They are also suitable occasions for offering new garments to the Deities.

Devotees observe many festivals by fasting up to a certain time and then feasting. They generally sing *bhajans* appropriate for the particular festival, as well as, of course, the Hare Kṛṣṇa *mahā-mantra*. For instance, on the disappearance day of a great Vaiṣṇava, devotees sing the song beginning *je ānilo prema-dhana*, which expresses the intense mood of separation from departed Vaiṣṇavas. Similarly, at festivals devotees read relevant passages and may also perform appropriate dramas. For instance, on Śrīla Bhaktisiddhānta Sarasvatī Ṭhākura's appearance day, they read or recite accounts of his transcendental activities. On Govardhana *Pūjā* day, they read the chapter entitled "Worshiping Govardhana Hill" from Śrīla Prabhupāda's book *Kṛṣṇa, the Supreme Personality of Godhead*. If there is a recorded lecture by Śrīla Prabhupāda speaking on a specific festival day, they may play that. (These recordings are available in a series called *Festivals with Śrīla Prabhupāda*.)

What follows is a list of some of the major festivals that ISKCON devotees observe, beginning with Gaura Pūrṇimā, which is the appearance anniversary of Lord Caitanya and the first day of the Gauḍīya Vaiṣṇava year. You can find the exact date of each festival in the ISKCON calendar; as with Ekādaśī, the dates are calculated according to the lunar calendar and thus vary each year on the Gregorian calendar.

Gaura Pūrṇimā

The appearance day of Lord Caitanya Mahāprabhu.

It generally occurs in March. There is fasting till moonrise, followed by Ekādaśī-type *prasāda*, and a feast at noon the next day. Read the account of Lord Caitanya's appearance in the *Caitanya-caritāmṛta*, *Ādi-līlā*, Chapter Thirteen. On Gaura Pūrṇimā and the days preceding it, thousands of devotees from all over the world congregate at ISKCON's Māyāpur center for a massive celebration that includes Navadvīpa-dhāma Parikramā (circumambulation of the holy places in Navadvīpa Dhāma).

Rāma-navamī

Appearance day of Lord Rāmacandra.

It generally occurs in April. There is fasting until sundown, then feasting. Read the account of Lord Rāma's pastimes in *Śrīmad-Bhāgavatam*, Canto 9, Chapters 10 and 11.

Nṛsiṁha Cāturdaśī

Appearance day of Lord Nṛsiṁhadeva.

It generally occurs in May. There is fasting until dusk, then feasting. Offer *panakam*, a drink made from cool water, jaggery, lemon juice, and ginger; this drink is Nṛsiṁhadeva's favorite. Read the account of His appearance in *Śrīmad-Bhāgavatam*, Canto 7, Chapter 8.

Ratha-yātrā

The day of Jagannātha *ratha-yātrā* in Purī.

It occurs in late June or early July. Devotees take the deities of Jagannātha, Subhadrā, and Balabhadra all together on one chariot, or separately on three chariots, through the city, all the while chanting the holy name and dancing. Śrīla Prabhupāda promoted this festival all over the world. Some ISKCON centers in India organize *ratha-yātrās* in their cities on the very day *ratha-yātrā* is celebrated in Purī; other centers throughout the world stage *ratha-yātrās* on other days of the year. Read *Śrī Caitanya-caritāmṛta*, *Madhya-līlā*, Chapter 13.

Jhulana-yātrā

A gorgeous five-day festival in which the Deities of Rādhā and Kṛṣṇa are placed on a swing, decorated profusely with flowers, and gently swung to and fro to the accompaniment of *kīrtana*. It generally occurs in early to mid August. A picture of Rādhā-Kṛṣṇa may also be swung.

Lord Balarāma's Appearance Day

The last day of Jhulana-yātrā is Lord Balarāma's Appearance Day. There is fasting till noon, then feasting.

Be sure to offer honey to Balarāma, since He is very fond of it. Read of Lord Balarāma's glories in *Caitanya-caritāmṛta, Ādi-līlā*, Chapter 5, and also appropriate passages from *Kṛṣṇa, the Supreme Personality of Godhead.*

Janmāṣṭamī

This appearance day of Lord Kṛṣṇa, is also known as Kṛṣṇāṣṭamī, Kṛṣṇa-jayantī and Gokulāṣṭamī. It generally occurs in August or early September. Devotees should fast and stay awake until midnight, and then honour Ekādaśī-style *prasāda*. Read extensively throughout the day from *Kṛṣṇa, the Supreme Personality of Godhead.*

Vyāsa-pūjā of Śrīla Prabhupāda

Śrīla Prabhupāda mercifully appeared in this world on Nandotsava, the day after Janmāṣṭamī. Devotees observe this event by worshiping Śrīla Prabhupāda with his Vyāsa-pūjā celebration, the most important festival of the year for all ISKCON members; for without Śrīla Prabhupāda's mercy none of us could have come to Kṛṣṇa consciousness.

Vyāsa-pūjā celebrations are conducted as follows: During the morning devotees fast and come together to hear and chant about Śrīla Prabhupāda and his glorious activities. Devotees may be tired from the previous day's Janmāṣṭamī observance, but on this special day they shake off their fatigue to glorify Śrīla Prabhupāda.

Devotees may read from biographical works on Śrīla Prabhupāda (such as *Śrīla Prabhupāda-līlāmṛta*) and from Vyāsa-pūjā books (special volumes of homages to Śrīla Prabhupāda that are compiled each year and offered to him on Vyāsa-pūjā). Also, on this day devotees often play recordings of Śrīla Prabhupāda's *bhajans* and lectures. Devotees speak about his glories and their appreciation of His Divine Grace.

At 11:40 or so, devotees offer a great feast simultaneously to the Deities and to Śrīla Prabhupāda. This offering is followed by *puṣpāñjali* (an offering of flowers at Śrīla Prabhupāda's *vyāsāsana*). Each devotee is given a large handful of flowers. One devotee recites the *guru-praṇāma mantras* (nama oṁ viṣṇu-pādāya, etc.) word by word. Word by word the assembled devotees repeat after the devotee leading. At the conclusion of each prayer, the leading devotee says, "*Puṣpāñjali!*" The assembled devotees repeat the word *puṣpāñjali* after him. Then everyone throws flowers as an offering at Śrīla Prabhupāda's lotus feet. Next all the devotees prostrate themselves before his deity or picture and offer obeisances. The whole procedure is repeated three times. After the *puṣpāñjali*, devotees hold an ecstatic *kīrtana* during the noon *ārati*, and finally *prasāda* is distributed.

All ISKCON devotees also observe the Vyāsa-pūjā of Śrīla Bhaktisiddhānta Sarasvatī Ṭhākura. Programs of fasting till noon and then feasting are also observed on the appearance days of Śrīla Gaurakiśora Dāsa Bābājī and Śrīla Bhaktivinoda Ṭhākura.

Rādhāṣṭamī

The appearance day of Śrīmatī Rādhārāṇī comes two weeks after Janmāṣṭamī. There is fasting till noon, then feasting. Śrīmatī Rādhārāṇī's favorite vegetable is *arbi* (Hindi name).

Read about Śrīmatī Rādhārāṇī in *Caitanya-caritāmṛta, Madhya-līlā*, Chapter 23, verses 86–92, and also in *Kṛṣṇa, the Supreme Personality of Godhead*, in the chapter "Deliverance of the Message of Kṛṣṇa to the Gopīs."

Vāmana Dvādaśī

The appearance of the Vāmana *avatāra*. Read from *Śrīmad-Bhāgavatam*, Canto 8, Chapters 18–22.

Govardhana Pūjā, Annakūṭa Mahotsava, and Gopūjā

These festivals are all observed on the same day, which generally comes in late October or early November. Devotees celebrate Govardhana *Pūjā* by worshiping Govardhana Hill. For Annakūṭa Mahotsava, they make a "Govardhana Hill" of *prasāda*, worship it, circumambulate it, and then distribute heaps of sumptuous *prasāda* to one and all. Gopūjā means "worship of the cows." See *Kṛṣṇa, the Supreme Personality of Godhead*, Volume 1, Chapters 24 and 25, and *Caitanya-caritāmṛta, Madhya-līlā*, Chapter 4, verses 67–75.

Disappearance day of Śrīla Prabhupāda

This festival generally comes just two days after Govardhana *Pūjā*. It is similar to Vyāsa-pūjā, but on this day the feeling of separation from our beloved Śrīla Prabhupāda is very strong. The disappearance days of Śrīla Bhaktisiddhānta Sarasvatī Ṭhākura, Śrīla Gaurakiśora Dāsa Bābājī, and Śrīla Bhakti vinoda Ṭhākura are all similarly observed. There is fasting until noon, and then feasting.

Disappearance festivals commemorate the passing of great Vaiṣṇavas from this world. Devotees celebrate them as festivals because in passing away a Vaiṣṇava shows how to finally conquer over *māyā* and enter the spiritual world.

Appearance of Advaita Ācārya

This festival generally occurs in late January or early February. There is fasting till noon, then feasting. See *Caitanya-caritāmṛta*, *Ādi-līlā*, Chapter 6.

Varāha Dvādaśī

This is the celebration of the appearance day of Lord Varāha. It generally occurs in February. See *Śrīmad-Bhāgavatam*, Canto 3, Chapters 13 and 18.

Nityānanda Trayodaśī

Appearance of Lord Nityānanda. It generally occurs in February. There is fasting till noon, then feasting. See *Caitanya-caritāmṛta*, *Ādi-līlā*, Chapter 5.

Obeisances

Offering obeisances is an important part of devotional service, by which the devotee confirms and reinforces his attitude of submission. Obeisances are especially meant for the Supreme Lord and His devotees.

One should offer obeisances by prostrating oneself on the ground, head down, or by placing the head, lower legs and forearms on the ground. One must also audibly offer specific prayers while bowing down.

When entering and leaving the temple room, one should offer obeisances to the Deities.

In all ISKCON temples is a *vyāsāsana* (formal raised seat for the spiritual master) upon which Śrīla Prabhupāda sits, in either his picture form or his deity form. The correct etiquette is to first offer obeisances to Śrīla Prabhupāda and then to the Deities on entering the temple room, and

vice versa while leaving. Offer obeisances to *Tulasī-devī* with the prayer *vṛndāyai tulasī-devyai priyāyai*, etc. (see section on Tulasī). Obeisances to Tulasī are generally offered at the time of *tulasī-ārati*, but one can offer them at other times also.

Offering obeisances to devotees is important in Kṛṣṇa consciousness because it enables us to make rapid advancement and also helps create and uphold loving relationships between devotees.

It is mandatory to offer obeisances to one's *guru* on entering and leaving his presence. Also, one should offer obeisances to a *sannyasi* at least the first time one sees him during the day. It is a good practice to offer obeisances individually to all devotees — particularly senior devotees — upon seeing them for the first time during the day.

One offers the *guru* obeisances with the particular *praṇāma-mantra* mentioning his name. The following *praṇāma-mantra* is used for other devotees:

vāñchā-kalpatarubhyaś ca kṛpā-sindhubhya eva ca
patitānāṁ pāvanebhyo vaiṣṇavebhyo namo namaḥ

"I offer my respectful obeisances unto all the Vaiṣṇava devotees of the Lord, who can fulfill the desires of everyone, just like desire trees, and who are full of compassion for the fallen souls."

In all ISKCON centers, devotees mutually offer obeisances to one another by bowing down and reciting this *mantra* in the morning, after *tulasī-ārati*.

Generally, when offered obeisances, a devotee returns them. One who is very senior in the community of devotees may not always return obeisances offered by those much junior. Rather, such senior devotees may offer blessings and good wishes for the other's spiritual advancement. This etiquette is particularly observed by *sannyasis* and initiating *gurus*.

If one ever speaks inconsiderate words or behaves improperly towards a Vaiṣṇava, he should, upon realizing his mistake, immediately offer obeisances to that Vaiṣṇava and beg for forgiveness. This is the proper thing to do, even if one considers that he has also been wronged by that Vaiṣṇava. Such behavior maintains sanctity and peace in the society of devotees.

Vaiṣṇava Appearance

Although dressing as a Vaiṣṇava is not essential (inward consciousness being more important than external appearance), it is important. Just as a policeman wears his uniform so that he will be recognized and dealt with as such, so a devotee dresses in devotee attire to proclaim to the world his commitment to Kṛṣṇa consciousness. Devotees who dress as such regularly have the pleasant experience of explaining to curious members of the public why they are devotees. Thus, dressing as devotees gives us more opportunities to preach.

Furthermore, by dressing as a Vaiṣṇava a devotee takes the responsibility to act as a Vaiṣṇava. One with the appearance of a *sadhu* is expected to conduct himself in a dignified way. So dressing as a devotee helps the devotee to act in an exemplary manner. If we look like Vaiṣṇavas, naturally we feel more like Vaiṣṇavas.

On the other hand, Western dress automatically tends to put us in a different frame of mind. Western dress is associated with Western standards, with a way of life based on lust and greed; therefore it is best avoided. If one feels uncomfortable appearing as a Vaiṣṇava in public, at least he can dress in devotee clothes at home, when visiting temples, or when practising Kṛṣṇa consciousness at home.

Standard Vaiṣṇava appearance is as follows:

For men

Tilaka, Tulasī neckbeads, shaved head with knotted *śikhā*, which should not be more than one and a half inches wide. Householders living outside the temple who feel constrained from keeping a shaved head may have very short, neatly kept hair, but not long hair, for long hair is considered objectionable by the followers of Caitanya Mahāprabhu. The face should be clean-shaven, with no beard, mustache, or sideburns. Except for sannyasis, one should wear the *dhotī* with a *kach* (the part of the *dhotī* tucked in at the back).

Brahmācārīs and *sannyasis* (celibate males who have dedicated their lives completely for Kṛṣṇa's service) wear saffron-coloured cloth (saffron being the colour of renunciation). Married men and unmarried men who have not committed themselves to ashram life wear white.

On the upper part of the body one should wear a traditional-style *kurtā*, or collarless buttoned shirt. T-shirts with nondevotional pictures or words are not suitable dress for Vaiṣṇavas.

Leather shoes, clothes, and bags should not be used.

Neatly attired, the Vaiṣṇava appears like a perfect aristocratic gentleman engaged in the service of Lord Kṛṣṇa.

For women

To uphold their chastity, women should dress conservatively. Traditional Indian dress (*sari*) is best, with *tilaka* and neckbeads. There should be no Western fashions, and the hair should be parted in the middle and braided. The rest of the body should be well covered in the presence of men other than one's husband and sons.

Holy Places

There are many important Vaiṣṇava pilgrimage sites throughout India, and even today pious Hindus frequent them. Such visits properly dovetail the propensity for travel and tourism. However, the scriptures advise that the main benefit to be derived from such visits to holy places is to associate with and hear from saintly persons residing there. Unfortunately, in the modern age, the importance of pilgrimage sites as places of spiritual instruction has been almost forgotten.

Gauḍīya Vaiṣṇavas know Māyāpur and Vṛndāvana as the two most important places in the whole universe (from the external viewpoint, they appear to be close to Calcutta and Delhi, respectively). Māyāpur is where Lord Caitanya appeared and performed pastimes in His youth, and Vṛndāvana is the place of Lord Kṛṣṇa's childhood pastimes. ISKCON has beautiful temples in both Māyāpur and Vṛndāvana, with facilities for visiting guests and devotees. At both these centers one can consult learned and advanced devotees on matters of spiritual knowledge. All devotees are invited to visit the ISKCON centers in Māyāpur and Vṛndāvana whenever they can.

According to scripture, any place where the Deity of Viṣṇu is installed, and especially where devotees are serving the Lord without personal motivation, is a great holy place. Therefore all ISKCON centers, even those in big cities, are holy places — places to get the *darśana* and blessings of Kṛṣṇa and His devotees and to render service. ISKCON centers regularly conduct seminars, courses, and training programs. Contact your nearest center for more information.

The Mood and Attitude of a Devotee

One of the most important statements in all of Śrīla Prabhupāda's books is found in the Preface to *The Nectar of Instruction*: "Advancement in Kṛṣṇa consciousness depends on the attitude of the follower."

This is a vast subject, but for beginners in Kṛṣṇa consciousness (and, indeed, for all devotees) two points are particularly important: humility and service attitude.

Śrīla Prabhupāda writes: "The complete path of *bhakti-yoga* is based on the process of becoming humble and submissive." (*Śrī Caitanya-caritāmṛta, Ādi-līlā* 7.148) And one of Lord Caitanya's most famous teachings is that a Vaiṣṇava should consider himself lower than a blade of grass. Such an exalted standard of humility is difficult to attain, yet as aspiring devotees we must try to cultivate this mood.

But often new devotees become falsely proud of what they consider their great spiritual advancement. It is not uncommon for devotees to be puffed up because they can sing *bhajans* or play *mṛdaṅga* expertly, because they have memorized some *ślokas*, because they come from a *brāhmaṇa* family, because they are academically qualified, or for some other foolish reason. But such pride is, on the contrary, an indication of lack of factual spiritual advancement. One who is actually interested in becoming a devotee of Kṛṣṇa must cast out this pride from the heart.

Another common obstacle for beginners in Kṛṣṇa consciousness is a poor service attitude. As fallen souls long conditioned by material illusion, we have lost our natural spirit of service to Kṛṣṇa. The whole purpose of taking to

Kṛṣṇa consciousness is to revive that dormant service spirit. Kṛṣṇa consciousness means service, transcendental loving service: service to Kṛṣṇa, service to *guru*, service to Vaiṣṇavas, service to the holy *dhāmas*, service to the holy names. Indeed, Śrīla Prabhupāda taught us that the Hare Kṛṣṇa mantra itself is a prayer to the Lord and His internal energy to be engaged in Their service.

We should be eager to render practical service to the Lord and His devotees. Whether it is cleaning the temple, cutting vegetables that will be cooked and offered to the Lord, managing Kṛṣṇa's temple, or preaching His glories, all services to Kṛṣṇa are spiritual and purifying. Whatever service we are asked to do, we should perform conscientiously and to the best of our ability. That will help us quickly advance in Kṛṣṇa consciousness. A lazy, half-hearted approach will not do.

The Kṛṣṇa consciousness movement is not meant for improving our financial position, enhancing our personal prestige, or providing a comfortable life. The aim is to become pure devotees of Kṛṣṇa and serve Him without any ulterior motive. To make rapid progress towards that goal, we must have a sound philosophical understanding of what Kṛṣṇa consciousness actually is. This understanding will develop in a devotee who regularly studies Śrīla Prabhupāda's books and seriously engages in devotional service with a humble mood.

Creating a Spiritual Atmosphere at Home

In Sanskrit there are two words for householders: *gṛhastha* and *gṛhamedhī*. The *gṛhastha*, though living with his wife and children, sees self-realization as the goal of his life. The *gṛhamedhī* doesn't — he's simply an ordinary materialistic person. A *gṛhastha's* home is called a *gṛhastha-āśrama*. It is an *āśrama* because it is meant for spiritual cultivation, the temple room being the most important place in the whole house.

Because the members of a *gṛhastha's* family feel themselves to be servants of Kṛṣṇa, they perform everything as an offering unto Him. They think, "This is not our home; it is Kṛṣṇa's. We are living here to serve Him. Everyone and everything here, including money, food, and so on, are meant only for His service."

Worshiping the Deity of Kṛṣṇa at home is especially conducive for cultivating such a devotional mood. Therefore Deity worship is essential for *gṛhasthas*, who are otherwise prone to fall into sense gratification. It is not that we keep a picture of Kṛṣṇa in one corner and use the rest of the house for our own purposes.

In order to spiritualize the home, keep pictures of Kṛṣṇa and His pure devotees throughout. It is better not to have pictures of demigods. Pictures of bogus *avatars*, Māyāvādī *gurus*, film stars, sports heroes, politicians, and the like have no place in a Kṛṣṇa conscious home and should be removed.

One way to powerfully spiritualize the home is to keep a full set of Śrīla Prabhupāda's books there. These books are literary incarnations of God and are as worshipable as Deities.

Television can be used for showing Kṛṣṇa conscious videos, but generally it is simply a disturbance. The TV is rightly called "the idiot box." It is an impersonal and brain-dulling medium. Studies suggest that excessive viewing, even of relatively serious material, can stunt intellectual and emotional development. TV has been a major factor in destroying family life in the West. The same thing is going on now in India and other countries. Certainly, home life centered on the TV cannot be very loving or happy. A major step, therefore, in making the home a suitable place to worship Kṛṣṇa is for the father to boldly remove the TV from the home. Sell it and get rid of it forever. The children may object, but for their own good, ignore their objections. Engage the family members in *pūjā*, *kīrtana*, and other activities of Kṛṣṇa consciousness, and they will soon forget TV.

Instead of listening to materialistic songs on the radio or other electronic devices, sing Vaiṣṇava *bhajans* and play bona fide *bhajan* cassettes and CDs.

Parents are duty-bound to train their children in Kṛṣṇa consciousness from a young age. The father has a special responsibility to serve as a *guru* for his wife and children.

Relating with Near and Dear Ones

Often, when one member of a family takes to Kṛṣṇa consciousness, all the other members of the family also become devotees. However, if other family members do not agree to become devotees, an awkward situation may develop. Sometimes, not only the family members but also friends and neighbors consider the new devotee crazy, harrass him, and accuse him of being ungrateful and irresponsible.

This is not something new. Eons ago, the demon Hiraṇyakaśipu severely harassed his son, the great devotee Prahlāda Mahārāja, just because Prahlāda would not relinquish his *viṣṇu-bhakti*.

Remembering Prahlāda, those who have developed even a slight taste for pure Kṛṣṇa consciousness cannot give it up for anything. A devotee may not be able to convince his relatives to take up Kṛṣṇa consciousness, but his relatives will also not be able to convince him to leave Kṛṣṇa consciousness.

Always consider the actual reality of existence: relationships with friends, country, family, and the rest are all fleeting. They are just like the bumping together of twigs floating in a river. Twigs sometimes join together in groups, then again, by the force of the current, they separate to form new groups. Similarly, in the mighty river of time we flit from one body to another. And in each body we take seriously our position as a dog, hog, human being, or whatever.

Another example is that of guests in a hotel who meet and start conversations but do not develop deep attachment for one another, knowing that they will all depart for different destinations after a fewdays.

In the materialistic way of life, one considers family attachments and family responsibilities all-important. Indeed, family life is the very basis of material existence (see *Śrīmad-Bhāgavatam* 5.5.8). But all devotees, even those who continue to live at home with their family members, should clearly recognize these family attachments for what they are: *māyā*.

Another consideration is that those who surrender themselves fully to Kṛṣṇa no longer have any familial or social duties to fulfill. *Śrīmad-Bhāgavatam* (11.5.41) clearly states this:

> *devarṣi-bhūtāpta-nṛṇāṁ pitṝṇāṁ*
> *na kiṅkaro nāyam ṛṇī ca rājan*
> *sarvātmanā yaḥ śaraṇaṁ śaraṇayaṁ*
> *gato mukundaṁ parihṛtya kartam*

"Anyone who has taken shelter of the lotus feet of Mukunda, the giver of liberation, giving up all kinds of obligation, and has taken to the path in all seriousness, owes neither duties nor obligations to the demigods, sages, general living entities, family members, humankind, or forefathers."

Indeed, a devotee who surrenders himself to the lotus feet of Kṛṣṇa does the best service to his family members, for Kṛṣṇa automatically grants liberation to many generations of a pure devotee's family (see *Śrīmad-Bhāgavatam* 7.10.18).

One should accept everything favorable for executing Kṛṣṇa consciousness and reject everything unfavorable. What is a favorable situation for one devotee may not be suitable for another. If our home life is not favorable for Kṛṣṇa consciousness, we should make every effort to make it so by trying to induce our family members to take up devotional service. At least we can try to get them to tolerate and respect our practice of *kṛṣṇa-bhakti*.

For those who are serious about Kṛṣṇa consciousness but are obliged to live in a home full of nondevotees, we can only recommend that they keep the peace as much as possible without compromising their principles. Often, such family members are actually good people in the ordinary moral sense, but we cannot expect that all will be fortunate enough to understand the paramount importance of Kṛṣṇa consciousness. Quite often, with patience and diligence a devotee is gradually able to turn apathetic or inimical family members toward devotional service.

In situations where, despite all efforts, family members remain rigidly inimical towards Kṛṣṇa consciousness, leaving home to take up the service of Kṛṣṇa full-time is an alternative that should be seriously considered and discussed with senior, responsible devotees. "A person whose main concern is Kṛṣṇa consciousness, even if he is entrapped in household life, should always be ready to leave household enticement as soon as possible." (*Śrīmad-Bhāgavatam* 3.23.49 purport)

Generally, however, it is not recommended that men with wives and dependent children suddenly leave home. But those who are over fifty years old, or younger men who are still unmarried, should seriously consider leaving home to join the association of devotees and thus practice Kṛṣṇa consciousness full-time. There is no need for them to unnecessarily spend all their lives at home, like ordinary materialistic people. "Vedic authority says that householders must leave home after the age of fifty." (*Śrīmad-Bhāgavatam* 3.24.35 purport)

One thing is certain: no one should give up his precious discovery of Kṛṣṇa consciousness under any circumstances, however difficult. Kṛṣṇa takes special care of those who serve Him under adverse conditions.

We should be determined to remain Kṛṣṇa conscious, even if our family members and friends don't understand us. Even if the whole world is against us, if Kṛṣṇa is on our side, we have nothing to lose or fear.

Man-Woman Association

puṁsaḥ striyā mithunī-bhāvam etaṁ
tayor mitho hṛdaya-granthim āhuḥ
ato gṛha-kṣetra-sutāpta-vittair
janasya moho 'yam ahaṁ mameti

"The attraction between male and female is the basic principle of material existence. On the basis of this misconception, which ties together the hearts of the male and female, one becomes attracted to his body, home, property, children, relatives, and wealth. In this way one increases life's illusions and thinks in terms of 'I and mine.'" (*Śrīmad-Bhāgavatam* 5.5.8)

In the modern age, free mixing between men and women is encouraged. However, traditional cultures around the world carefully restricted association between the sexes. Without such precautions, basic morality cannot be maintained. Kṛṣṇa conscious persons are advised to be careful in this regard. Even among devotees, it is best to keep men and women separate as much as possible.

Vedic culture restricts association between men and women not only for *brahmacārīs* and *sannyasis* but even for married couples. Of course, within marriage husband and wife must associate, but that association should be only to assist each other in advancement in Kṛṣṇa consciousness. Unnecessary mixing, even between husband and wife, is the cause of falldown for both. (This subject has been elaborately discussed by the author in his book *Brahmacarya in Kṛṣṇa Consciousness*)

Kṛṣṇa conscious couples sanctify their conjugal relationship by uniting for the purpose of begetting devotee children. Śrīla Prabhupāda directed his householder disciples, both men and women, to chant at least fifty rounds of the Hare Kṛṣṇa *mahā-mantra* to purify their minds before sexual union. What kind of soul is attracted to the womb of the mother depends on the consciousness of the parents at the time of union. So if the parents are Kṛṣṇa conscious when they conceive a child, he or she will have a strong inclination for Kṛṣṇa consciousness.

In this modern, disturbed age, it is often difficult for husband and wife to live peacefully together. But if Kṛṣṇa consciousness replaces selfish sense gratification as the basis of marriage, family life can be pure and happy.

A full discussion of married life in Kṛṣṇa consciousness is beyond the scope of this book. Those who would like to spiritualize their family life should contact mature, senior *gṛhastha* members of ISKCON for guidance and advice.

Become a Member of ISKCON

All over the world people with similar interests form organizations and work together to fulfill their common aims. For instance, businessmen form chambers of commerce and workmen form labor unions. Similarly, Śrīla Prabhupāda formed the International Society for Krishna Consciousness for people who are interested in understanding Kṛṣṇa.

There are different types of membership within ISKCON. Full-time dedicated devotees join the society's ashrams and submit themselves to the discipline of devotional life. They work hard all day for Kṛṣṇa and ask nothing in remuneration.

Of course, the society takes care of their food, clothing, lodging, and other basic needs. Many thousands of such dedicated workers are needed. Full-time devotees in ISKCON receive training in *pūjā*, *bhajans*, *kīrtana*, *mantras*, philosophy, cooking, self-dependence, and spiritual leadership. But the most important item of all is training in a service attitude in Kṛṣṇa consciousness, training in how to surrender to Kṛṣṇa. Those interested in surrendering their lives to Kṛṣṇa should contact their nearest ISKCON center.

Of course, it is also wholly possible to prosecute Kṛṣṇa consciousness seriously at home. By following the instructions given in this book everyone can achieve all perfection, even while living at home.

Those with sufficient financial means can become Life Members of ISKCON by payment of a fixed donation.

And if you do not feel ready to take up any of the roles outlined above, we request that you at least take up the regular chanting of the *mahā-mantra*:

Hare Kṛṣṇa, Hare Kṛṣṇa,
Kṛṣṇa Kṛṣṇa, Hare Hare
Hare Rāma, Hare Rāma,
Rāma Rāma, Hare Hare

Words from Śrīla Prabhupāda

Secrets of Success

The process of *bhakti-yoga* is simultaneously very difficult and very easy to perform...[For] a sincere person devotional service is very easy. But for one who is not determined and sincere, this process is very difficult. [*Śrīmad-Bhāgavatam* 4.8.30 purport]

* * *

Anyone can become successful in devotional service provided he displays no duplicity...[One] must be very frank and open-minded (*amāyinaḥ*). To be situated in a lower status of life is not a disqualification for success in devotional service. The only qualification is that whether one is a *brāhmaṇa*, *kṣatriya*, *vaiśya*, or *śūdra*, he must be open, frank, and free from reservations. Then, by performing his particular occupational duty under the guidance of a proper spiritual master, he can achieve the highest success in life. As confirmed by the Lord Himself, *striyo vaiśyās tathā śūdrās te 'pi yānti paraṁ gatim* (*Bhagavad-gītā* 9.32). It does not matter what one is, whether a *brāhmaṇa*, *kṣatriya*, *vaiśya*, *śūdra*, or a degraded woman. If one engages himself seriously in devotional service, working with body, mind, and intelligence, he is sure to be successful in going back home, back to Godhead. [*Śrīmad-Bhāgavatam* 4.21.33 purport]

* * *

Remain enthusiastic.
Be confident of success.
Follow the regulative principles.
Be staightforward.
Keep the association of devotees.
Be patient.
Do not become morose.
And Kṛṣṇa will surely help you.
[Instructions to residents of New Tālavan, spoken in Dallas in 1975]

About the Author

Born of British parents in England in 1957, the author joined ISKCON in 1975 in London and was initiated that year, with the name Ilāpati dāsa, by the founder-*ācārya*, His Divine Grace A.C. Bhaktivedanta Swami Prabhupāda.

From 1977 to 1979 Ilāpati dāsa was based in India, mostly traveling in West Bengal distributing Śrīla Prabhupāda's books. He spent the following ten years helping to pioneer ISKCON's preaching in Bangladesh, Burma, Thailand, and Malaysia.

In 1989 he was granted the order of *sannyāsa*, receiving the name Bhakti Vikāsa Swami, and again made his base in India. He has since traveled widely throughout the subcontinent, lecturing in English, Hindi, and Bengali.

Bhakti Vikāsa Swami also preaches in other parts of the world, and continues to write books and magazine articles. His books have been translated into more than fifteen languages.

GLOSSARY

A

Ācārya — spiritual master who has realized the import of *śāstra* and by practice and precept establishes religious principles; *guru.*

Ārati — a ceremony of worship performed with chanting of *mantras* and offerings of items such as ghee lamps, fans, flowers, and incense.

Āśrama — ashram.

B

Bhajana — devotional song.

Bhakti — See Devotional service.

Bhoga — items such as foodstuffs or flowers specifically meant to be offered for the Lord's enjoyment.

Brahmācārī — member of the first (brahmacarya) order of Vedic spiritual life, i.e., a celibate student of a spiritual master.

Brāhmaṇa — (1) learned, spiritually advanced priest or teacher; (2) often erroneously designates a certain caste, or members thereof, claiming to be *brāhmaṇas* on the basis of heredity alone.

C

(Śrī) Caitanya Mahāprabhu — (1486–1534) Supreme Lord who appeared as His own devotee to teach love of Himself, especially by the process of congregational chanting of His holy names. Also known as Lord Caitanya.

D

Demigods — personalities residing in the higher planets, principal among whom are assigned by the Supreme Lord to oversee the affairs of the universe and are worshiped for material boons by materialistic followers of Vedic culture.

Devotional service — the process of worshiping Śrī Kṛṣṇa, the Supreme Personality of Godhead, by dedicating one's thoughts, words, and actions to Him in loving submission. See Kṛṣṇa consciousness.

Dhāma — transcendental abode of the Lord, eternally existing as the spiritual world beyond the material universes and also manifested within the material world as certain holy places such as Navadvīpa-dhāma and Vṛndāvana-dhāma.

G

Gāyatrī — *mantra* recited within the mind at sunrise, midday, and sunset by suitably initiated persons.

Gṛhastha — married person acting in accordance with Vedic religious principles for the sake of spiritual elevation.

Gopīcandana — yellow rock from Dvārakā (a holy place in India), from which a paste is made and applied as tilaka. See Tilaka.

Gurukula — Vedic school for boys.

H

Hare Kṛṣṇa mahā-mantra — great incantation for deliverance: Hare Kṛṣṇa, Hare Kṛṣṇa, Kṛṣṇa Kṛṣṇa, Hare Hare/Hare Rāma, Hare Rāma, Rāma Rāma, Hare Hare.

Harināma — the holy name of Hari (Kṛṣṇa) and the chanting thereof.

I

ISKCON — International Society for Krishna Consciousness. Founded in 1966 in New York by His Divine Grace A.C. Bhaktivedanta Swami Prabhupāda, it is the principle manifestation of what is popularly known as the Hare Krishna movement.

J

Japa — soft recitation of the Lord's holy names on beads. See also Hare Kṛṣṇa mahā-mantra.

Japa-mālā — string of beads used for counting japa. See also Tulasī.

K

Karatālas — hand cymbals played in *kīrtana.*

Kīrtana — chanting the names and glories of the Supreme Lord; usually used to indicate singing His names. See also Hare Kṛṣṇa mahā-mantra; *Saṅkīrtana.*

Kṛṣṇa (Krishna) — the original, all-attractive form of the Supreme Personality of Godhead.

Kṛṣṇa consciousness — acting in knowledge of one's relationship with Kṛṣṇa, the Supreme Absolute Truth. See also Devotional service.

M

Mahā-mantra — See Hare Kṛṣṇa *mahā-mantra.*

Mālā — (1) garland, string of beads, necklace, rosary; (2) 108 recitations of the mahā-mantra, counted on a string of 108 beads. See also Japa-mālā, Tulasī.

Maṅgala-ārati — first *ārati* ceremony of the day, performed before dawn. See *Ārati.*

Māyā — an energy of the Supreme Lord, in the material sphere personified as His deluding potency. (lc)-illusion; forgetfulness of one's eternal relationship as servant of God, Kṛṣṇa.

Māyāpur — appearance place of Śrī Caitanya Mahāprabhu; according to modern political considerations, presently in West Bengal, India. The site of ISKCON's world headquarters.

Māyāvāda — the philosphical thesis that the Absolute Truth is formless and impersonal or void, and the infitesimal living entity is equal to that Absolute Truth.

Māyāvādī — follower of Māyāvāda philosophy.

Mṛdaṅga — two-headed drum used to accompany *saṅkīrtana.*

N

Navadvīpa — sacred area comprising nine islands within one of which Māyāpur is situated, and within another, the present town of Navadvip. See Māyāpur.

Nṛsiṁha(deva) — half-man, half-lion incarnation of Lord Kṛṣṇa.

P

Paramparā — chain of succession from *guru* to disciple to granddisciple, and so on, through which transcendental knowledge is conveyed.

Prasādam — "mercy"; food remnants or other items received as mercy from the Supreme Lord or His topmost devotees; usually refers to items offered in arcana to the Lord for His pleasure.

Pūjā — (1)formal worship.

Pūjārī — "one who performs *pūjā*"; *brāhmaṇa* engaged in the worship of the Lord's Deity form.

S

Sādhana — a means to attain a spiritual goal; regulated spiritual practice.

Sādhu — (1) saintly person, especially a renunciant; (2) devotee of Kṛṣṇa, especially a pure devotee or renunciant; (3) Hindu holy man.

Sahajiyā — aberrant performer of devotional activities who neglects prescribed rules and regulations and whose philosophical understanding is deviant.

Saṅkīrtana — congregational chanting of the Supreme Lord's holy names. See also Hare Kṛṣṇa mahā-mantra; *Kīrtana.*

Śāstra — revealed scripture; the four *Vedas* and literature in pursuance of the Vedic version.

Śikhā — tuft of hair on the back of the head by Vaiṣṇavas and most other sects within Vedic society.

Śikṣā — training, education, instruction.

Śloka — Sanskrit verse, usually from a recognized scripture or text.

Śrī — prepositioned term used as an honorific address or to denote reverence for a sacred book, place, or other object.

Śrīla Prabhupāda — founder-*ācarya* of the International Society for Krishna Consciousness and the greatest preacher of Kṛṣṇa consciousness in the modern age.

Śrīmad-Bhāgavatam — the topmost Vedic literature, it gives confidential and definitive understanding of Lord Kṛṣṇa, His devotees, and pure devotional service to Him.

T

Tilaka — auspicious clay markings placed by devotees on the forehead and eleven other parts of the body.

Tulasī — (1) sacred plant most dear to Lord Kṛṣṇa and thus worshiped by the Lord's devotees; (2) in her original form, a gopī of Vṛndāvana. Tulasī wood is utilized in two kinds of beads essential to Gauḍīya Vaiṣṇavas: neckbeads and chanting beads (*japa-mālā*). Her leaves are essential in offering bhoga to Lord Kṛṣṇa, who does not accept any offering sans tulasī leaves.

V

Vaiṣṇava — devotee of Viṣṇu, Lord Kṛṣṇa.

Viṣṇu — (1) Supreme Lord; (2) Lord Kṛṣṇa's expansions in Vaikuṇṭha; (3) His expansions for the creation and maintenance of the material universes.

Vṛndāvana — (1) topmost transcendental abode of the Supreme Lord, Kṛṣṇa; (2) the same abode descended at the site of the present town of Vrindaban, India, situated about one hundred kilometres southeast of Delhi, in which He enacted childhood pastimes five thousand years ago.